InCite

To Ruthie —
Eureka! ☺
Scott Ski — 2008 —

By Scott Ski

Panache Publishing

ISBN 978-0-9797889-0-1

Proudly Manufactured in the United States of America

Second Edition

Additional copies of InCite may be purchased at: **ScottSki.net**

InCite

Table of Contents

*Historical source material is available online at **ScottSki.net/InCite***

My sincere Thanks…

to the Good Lord ~ the source of all Insight and InCite

and to the Rustuen family for their faithful love and support.

Deepest Thanks, as always, to Robbi

This book

is dedicated to *Colonel Taz,* my Siberian Husky.

His challenging personality inspired my first book

<u>**Dogged and Determined**</u>

and set me on the path toward <u>InCite</u>.

InCite

Why InCite?

The fast-paced, future driven world surrounding us offers little time to contemplate, and even less time to garner or share the significant insights of life.

Yet it is insight that enables us to set the sails as the Captain of our seas rather than becoming the rudderless boat driven by those same seas.

Insight enables incite; the astuteness to act rather than merely react to the constantly changing, demanding world that envelops us.

This little book offers a collection of short, quick opportunities for such contemplation.

Scott Ski

"Those who cannot remember the past

are condemned to repeat it."

George Santayana -- Harvard professor, 1905

1
In Plain Sight
1979-80 C.E

Breathtaking and enigmatic, the Andes Mountains of Peru in South America stand shrouded in mist and mystery. Hidden from the world at 8,000 feet above the sea, this rugged land conceals the long forgotten remnants of the great Inca Empire. Behind towering peaks nestle the aged and eroded remains of Cuzco, the Inca capital. One hundred miles from Cuzco across the uneven, craggy landscape sits the sequestered and elaborate city of Machu Piccu. Cloaked in legend before its contemporary re-discovery in 1911, the abandoned city sprawls haunting, alluring, and perplexing amidst soaring summits and veiled valleys.

Hewn from huge granite rocks now ancient and crumbled, great long walls once snaked from snow-crested mountaintops down the slopes to Machu Piccu, Cuzco and throughout the empire. Intricate channels chiseled into the blocks had long vanished into debris. Occasionally discernable, long-deserted dirt foot roads still attempt to unite the far-flung realm. Overgrown with vegetation, slowly reclaimed by the natural environment over time, the scattered remains linger in mute testimony of a wealthy, past culture.

In the 1520's, at the height of the Inca civilization, the bustling town of Patallacta stood strategically placed midway between Machu Piccu and Cuzco. A commerce and transit hub, the borough served as the overnight rest stop for travelers on their trek between these two thriving cities. Patallacta prosperity depended upon the continued success of the two population centers. Following the empire's collapse the two metropolises fell into ruin. Patallacta and her residents continued, lapsing into severe poverty.

Half a millennium passed. In present times, the isolated, mountain shantytown of Patallacta still huddles between the two long, abandoned cities of the Inca, and under the shadow of a forsaken wall. The little hamlet has struggled here five hundred years, its few remaining inhabitants barely subsisting in the parched, barren, unforgiving land. Nothing would grow during the five month dry season. These Peruvian families have eked out their meager existence amidst hardship and deprivation. Life continues as it has for the last fifteen generations. Patallacta with its difficulties has always been their lot. Time seems to have stood still in this place.

In 1979, Patallacta's inhabitants watched inquisitively as new visitors arrived at their village. A multi-national team of archaeologists had received funding to excavate long forgotten, ancient sites in the region. The team searched diligently for shards of history to gain insight into the vast, rich, albeit short-lived Inca Empire; a civilization long believed to have only reigned in the realm of myth.

As Patallacta happened to be near one of the major archeological digs, the inhabitants watched the proceedings with increasing interest. Some of the residents, hired by the scientists to gather, dig, sift, and carry the uncovered artifacts began to hear the stories of their Inca ancestors. As the work progressed more information emerged. History unfolded; slices of the tremendous heritage of the Inca civilization and Patallacta's forbearers. In listening to the scientists, the local people discovered intriguing snippets of their great legacy. Slowly the stacked wall rocks strewn about the village generated intense interest. Never before had the wrecked edifices conveyed significance. The people became conscious that here existed dozens of crumbling, overgrown and broken stone canals. Now they saw…and understood the personal application in the history that had been surrounding them.

This insight into the past incited them to act. The villagers diligently searched, carefully rediscovered and painstakingly rebuilt the half-millennium old water systems and terraced fields of the ancient Incas. Hundreds of years of neglect and overgrowth gave way when met with vigor and human determination. Some villagers took assignments to free the canal troughs from debris. Others cleared and planted the terraces. Fresh water glacier streams soon began to quench the parched soil and the town for the first time in half a millennium, extending Patallacta's growing season. That following fall, the village celebrated a bountiful harvest, rich in the promise of a budding future.

By listening to the past and responding, the people dramatically improved their quality of life. The solution had lain scattered before them for generation after generation after generation…hundreds of years. The key to their ages-old dilemma had been in plain sight the entire time. The townsfolk however, having lost their past, repeated a cycle, never realizing their forgotten heritage held the secret to prosperity and a better life. Ignorance had been their lot for 500 years and that ignorance resulted in increasing poverty with each subsequent generation.

The tools for our success, the building blocks for our improvement, often lay scattered about us in the lessons of the past, if we would take the time to understand and use them…for insight and incite.

2
A Bent Piece of Metal
1206 -1226 C.E.

From the obscure, windswept bleakness of the Gobi desert emerged Temujin, a 44-year-old warrior and his cobbled together confederacy of small tribes. In the year 1206, this illiterate nomad from nowhere, leading a band of "nobodies" swept across the Asian Steppes and quickly conquered everything in their path.

Although not massive in number, their superb horsemanship, fleetness across the landscape, and devastating quickness in confrontation made them unstoppable. Temujin's troops proved so mobile they gave the impression of materializing everywhere and seemingly all at once. Encouraging the illusion, Temujin created a name that elicited the image of a vast, overwhelming force. He called his cavalry "the Horde".

Art and writings of the period describe Temujin's horsemen in awed and mystical terms. Legends arose that the Horde lived, ate and slept on horseback. They became "at one" with their diminutive steeds. The swiftness and maneuverability of this cavalry stood unparalleled. Facing forward, sideways or sitting backwards in the saddle, they could accurately shoot a bow…at full gallop. They never suffered defeat in battle.

Within 20 years Temujin hammered out an empire that would eventually extend from Hungary in the west to Korea in the east and from northern Siberia to India…the largest land empire in history; an empire that lasted over two and a half centuries.

Most of us know Temujin better from history's name for him with a title akin to Emperor or King. Temujin was called the "Universal Leader of Men", which in the Mongol language translates to "Genghis Khan".

How did an illiterate, unknown group of nobodies from nowhere manage to take over the known world? One great secret to Genghis Khan's success lay in his mounted riders' control and ability to fully use one piece of technology that no one else in the world possessed; an invention consisting of a long, simple piece of bent metal. One of these bent-metal, elongated hoops hung on each side of the saddle, suspended by a leather strap. The rider's feet placed firmly in the hoops offered tremendous stability and control while on horseback.

Neither European knights, clanking heavily aboard their massive Destrier mounts, nor Asian horsemen utilizing unwieldy, wooden footholds could match the amazing speed and maneuverability brought by the Mongol Horde to battle. Thus a simple piece of metal, the *long stirrup*, significantly changed the history of the world.

So often we hear…and actually believe that we can never change the world. But don't ever acquiesce. Keep working at it. A simple solution, well used, can become the leading edge of sophistication in almost any avenue of endeavor.

And when people scoff, as they often do, simply remember the story of how a bent piece of metal changed the world.

And smile confidently.

3
Appomattox
April 9, 1965 C.E.

On the morning of April 9, 1865, Civil War Confederate General Robert E. Lee put on his finest dress uniform, mounted his white steed, Traveler, and quietly rode away from his tired and tattered troops toward Appomattox, where he would surrender his beaten army to the Union Forces of General Ulysses S. Grant. As Lee rode to meet his conqueror, he fully expected his men would be herded like cattle into railroad cars and hauled away to meet their dire fates in a Union prison. He as their general would be tried and executed as a disgraced traitor to his country.

Pulling up his horse before the appointed meeting place, General Lee steeled himself to meet his fate honorably and attempted to quell the deep concern for his loyal troops. In the tidy living room of the home where the vanquished and the victor met, the two leaders sat in simple chairs on either side of a small round table. Lee asked General Grant what his terms of surrender were to be. Grant simply told Lee that his men were free to return to their families, taking their horses and personal weapons with them. Go home to their farms to rebuild their lives. Furthermore, Lee too was free to go home and create a peaceful life outside of the military.

As an officer and a gentleman steeped in military tradition, Lee offered Grant his sword, the official sign of subservience and surrender. Grant politely refused it. General Lee heaved a deep sigh. He had come expecting to be derided, humiliated, disgraced and probably put to death. Instead the Confederate commander would leave with dignity, honor and life for himself and his valiant soldiers. As the Union general watched General Lee mount Traveler and then turn the horse to ride back to his troops, General Grant slowly removed his hat and solemnly saluted his defeated enemy. It was a most generous gesture of respect. As he glanced back, that moment forever etched itself into Lee's memory.

The entire affair and especially this final act of graciousness deeply affected the defeated general. As long as he lived, Lee allowed absolutely no critical word of Grant ever to be spoken in his presence. Because of General Grant's benevolence, thousands of lives were spared, hundreds of families reunited. Instead of being reviled, executed and forgotten, Robert E. Lee became an educator and college president, revered as a great individual and noble leader...even in defeat.

Most important of all, Grant's generosity started the nation on the path to healing from the great wounds of the nation's most terrible war. The United States had nearly been ripped apart at the seams by the conflict. General Grant had every right to handle the surrender even as Lee himself had anticipated. No one would have questioned it; the destruction and enormous human toll caused by the confederacy rebellion had been extreme, the greatest loss of American life in any war. The urge to play the role of ultimate victor must have tugged intensely at Grant.

However General Grant looked beyond the emotional gratification of destroying his enemy to what would be the best solution for the United States. He recognized that while on opposite sides of the war, he and Lee were alike with passion for that same country. Grant chose to trust General Lee and his men with the terms of peace, and to treat them with the respect he knew he would wish for his own men. Graciousness in victory and triumph may have done more to eventually re-unite the country than the brutal battles that preceded it.

May we truly seek to be gracious and respectful in all our victories in life.

4
Pesky Decisions
1969 C.E.

Amidst the political turbulence of Southeast Asia in the late 1960's the newly formed nation of Malaysia sprang forth. Consisting of the northern third of the island of Borneo plus the tail-end of Thailand's peninsula, the young nation sought recognition apart from its South China Sea neighbors, Thailand, Brunei, Vietnam and Indonesia.

Malaysia sought to earn prominence, stability and wealth through its export of natural resources particularly its exotic woods, mahogany and teak. Lush tropical climate graced the country with a dense and massive vegetation of jungles and forests. Very quickly Malaysia also sought the tourism market and began presenting itself as a garden paradise.

As incursions into the forests and jungles for industry, housing and tourism grew, a confrontation developed between man and mosquito. With human populations expanding into wilderness areas, the discomfort and disease presented by the pesky bugs threatened the government's scope and vision. Not wanting to slow the pace of their plans the administration needed a solution to occur quickly.

Still seeking global acceptance, they deemed that using science to resolve the problem would enable Malaysia to garner respect among the industrialized nations. Turning to technology the government decided to solve the issue using the current and common remedy: spraying the infested areas with the highly potent pesticide DDT, D(ICHLORO)D(IPHENYL)T(RICHLOROETHANE.

Even in the densest jungles, the bug killer worked exceptionally well. Infestations quickly scaled way back. The results also turned into literal feasts for the legions of cockroaches which existed throughout the region. These pests suddenly received a major food boon and happily devoured what appeared to them as mountains of dead mosquitoes.

However DDT does not perish with its intended target. The powerful toxin retains its potency continuing to kill as it travels through each successive victim. Soon masses of dead and dying cockroaches littered the landscape, demonstrating to the government it had gleaned an additional bonus.

This windfall did not go unnoticed by the region's large lizard population. The geckos actively and eagerly consumed the piles of deceased roaches. In an odd twist of genetic science the geckos did not die from the residual poison, but their central nervous systems were greatly affected. The lizards slowed down to the speed of old land turtles.

The region's cats immediately pounced upon this delightful turn of events. Here was something new to capture the attention of the curiosity-driven cats. Now they were able to enjoy teasing then eating the suddenly slow-moving lizards. Of course the primary purpose of cats in the Malaysian scheme of life was not to taunt the normally lightening-fast lizards but instead to actively destroy and devour the overwhelming wealth of rats. But the cats opted for the easier prey of demented lizards and the nation's felines proceeded to perish in large quantities. Fewer cats meant massively more rats, and the country's rat population soared along with the health horrors inherent.

With the escalating dilemma moving up the food chain, the World Health Organization intervened, banning the DDT. In an effort to restore the ecological balance, the Malaysian government realized it now needed replenishment to offset the deficiency. They engaged in history's largest feline airlift. Scouring and scrounging numerous countries in the Asian region and beyond, the government teams amassed planeloads of cats for import to Malaysia. Their mission: to kill the rats.

What appears reasonable for one situation could wreak havoc in ways never anticipated for another. In an increasingly fast paced world there arises the rush and roar to race ahead without weighing or testing actions. The urge to make quick assumptions, snap judgments, and split second decisions may produce pressured, deficient and poorly controlled plans. Decisions that can return to haunt in ways more varied, more intense and more costly than the original vexation.

Weigh decisions well before proceeding. Lugging a problem twice or beyond can exact a far heavier, painful toll.

5
Hanna's Dangerous Mission
April, 1945 C.E.

Hanna had schooled as a medical missionary to aid the native tribes in Africa. To reach these intractable lands Hanna decided to train as a pilot, a lofty choice for any woman in the male-dominated world of 1932. Hanna however proved intrepid, resolute in her quest to acquire the sky. Once airborne her life changed dramatically as Hanna discovered both her greatest skill and absolute passion.

Bold and fearless, Hanna quickly rose to become a formidable aviatrix through the 1930's and into the 1940's. She was the first woman to fly a helicopter, initially outdoors, and later in an amazing feat within an aircraft hanger during a major European air show. Hanna triumphed as the first female to fly a glider over the Swiss Alps. She ranks among the earliest women test pilots, piloting experimental rocket interceptor planes and test craft described as "flying bombs with a cockpit." She test-flew the world's first jet fighter. Hanna set more than 40 altitude, speed and endurance records in a variety of powered and non-powered aircraft during her career. Like any great daredevil, she found herself fortunate to be alive after many of her flights. She proudly boasted she had broken every bone in her body at one time or another. One of only two women ever to do so, Hanna earned the highest civilian and military honor her country had to offer.

Hanna fully realized the risk and sacrifice required to achieve one's goals. In late April 1945, the Chief of the Air Force had been declared a traitor during wartime. The presence of his replacement, General Robert Griem, was required immediately in the capital city to receive official deputation and the new war strategies. This likely-suicidal mission, flying across enemy-held territory to deliver the general and later escape with him required a dauntless individual. Only a pilot with the skills developed in Hanna's thirteen years of audacious aviation prowess would risk the undertaking. Hanna stepped forward to request the challenge.

In her mind this air-run entailed a second and deeply personal mission. Hanna sought to achieve the rescue of a prominent leader she greatly idolized. Trapped in the besieged city of their destination, he would be surely captured by hostile forces if not removed. Supremely confident, Hanna believed herself to be the ace flyer who could successfully attempt an endeavor to liberate him.

In short time, the swift fighter plane containing Hanna and the general raced along beneath the supporting air cover of 40 heavily armed fighter aircraft. Hordes of hostile Russian forces soon intercepted their squadron. Dodging, swooping and roaring at top speed, the duo careened over and under the mass of aerial dogfights screaming and soaring around them. As planes furiously fought, exploded, and fell on all sides, Griem and Hanna slipped through the fray. While the two landed the safety of Gatow airfield, what was left of the cover force defended them against fresh fighter planes.

At dusk, Griem and Hanna quickly boarded a Storch, a smaller and lighter plane, stealthily skimming the landscape to avoid detection. Enemy guns discovered them, damaging the aircraft. General Griem, piloting the plane, sustained shrapnel wounds to his foot and leg. With her skill, Hanna reached over his shoulders and took the controls, hedgehopping across the miles of enemy held territory to elude the ground gunners. Hanna deftly landed the plane amidst flames, rubble and smoldering ruins at her destination. She quickly hid her craft on a bombed out city street. With the fire of battle raging nearby, she helped the general hustle to safe fortifications.

Protected within the national headquarters, General Griem immediately received his promotion and the new directions to advance the war. His wounds required him to rest for two days before flying. Hanna recognized her opportunity to achieve her personal objective...yet after two days spent pleading with the country's leader, she could not convince him to leave. Instead, Hanna witnessed a person far removed from the dynamic image and unwavering determination she had always admired. Believing his own time had come to an end, he ordered Hanna and the general to go and continue the fight against their enemies. It was for Hanna to return and to aid the success of the future.

Distraught and confused, Hanna bid the leader she so idolized a heartfelt farewell. She had to survive, to carry on and follow his charge to her. Wincing under the thunder of booming artillery and the sharp staccato of weapons fire ringing in her ears, Hanna raced through the darkness of the evening to her light plane, swung it about and helped the injured general aboard. She leapt in and started the engine. Checking that her vital cargo, the new Air Force Chief, was safely loaded in the back of the small craft, she skillfully negotiated the rubble and crater-strewn boulevard. Dodging the volleys of small arms shots as she crossed into Russian-held streets, the plane managed to attain airspeed. Stung in the glare of harsh enemy searchlights the aircraft shuddered and echoed with the ricochets and near misses of intense weapons fire. Managing to stay aloft, Hanna's craft held the distinction of being the last to escape the invaded city. Maneuvering just above the tree tops, Hanna, the aviatrix extraordinaire, adroitly evaded the anti-aircraft batteries and swarms of hostile fighter planes patrolling the skies.

Successfully, Hanna Reitsch and General Robert Griem finally reached their airbase, but Hanna arrived weeping and inconsolable. On this spring day in April of 1945, she had failed in her greatest and most epic effort: to save the one person she esteemed most in the world…Adolf Hitler. Hanna was devastated.

Seven months later, following the end of the war, Hanna Reitsch gave testimony to Allied military officials. She stated that after her many years of adulation, those two days of close, personal time with Hitler revealed him to be a far different person than publicly presented by the Third Reich. She concluded her statement advising that no one should ever possess the kind of total power Hitler once wielded.

Failure or success? The perception often blurs and crosses. Hanna Reitsch failed miserably in her mission, yet her failure would be widely viewed as a success to the rest of the world, a good fortune later recognized by Hanna herself.

Like two ends of a rope, failure and success may appear opposite. However the tightly braided strands creating one end are the same, long fibers stretching to the other. Upon careful examination, one can discover the threads of both, success and failure, deeply intertwined within any situation.

Depending on one's point of view, in every failure can be found the filaments of success.

6
Setting the Pace
17ᵗʰ Century C.E.

A brilliant orange, setting sun was just alighting upon the treetops as the little ferry raft approached the far side of the great river. The renowned 17ᵗʰ Century, Ming Dynasty artist, Chou Yung and his young, adolescent assistant began gathering up their piles of original artwork, irreplaceable documents and valuable sketch books that they were scheduled to present to prospective patrons the following day in the nearby town. Since paper, ink and literate assistance proved a scant commodity during those times; prominent individuals carried a multitude of original documents, official paperwork, certificates, letters and artworks to substantiate their identity, ability and credibility. Being an artist, Chou literally carried his work and reputation wherever he journeyed. He even employed an apprentice to assist with the load.

By the time the boat docked and the pair stepped ashore, the tall trees nearly obscured the rapidly setting sun. Daylight intermittently peeked through the leaves, the branches gently swaying as the late day breezes picked up.

"Can we make it to the town before dark?" inquired Chou Yung of the boatman. Apprehension in his voice combined with worrisome glances toward the sunset, revealed his genuine concern. Towns were walled fortresses in those times. Because the untamed and vast countryside swarmed freely with bandits, the town gates closed at dusk for security and protection. Not reaching the safety of a protected settlement before dark meant a fearful night involving the wilderness, along with the grave peril of falling prey to the brigands.

The old, wizened boatman squinted at the horizon. "The town is about a mile away..." he offered as he glanced at the two travelers. Noting the loosely bundled art sketches and delicately rolled documents stacked in their arms, he offered some advice. "Yes, you can make it to the town before dark, but only if you do not walk too fast."

In their overriding concern to reach safety, Chou Yung and his companion heard the boatman's remark, comprehending only the estimate of a mile distance. Glancing at each other, the duo shrugged off the admonition to walk as rather absurd and illogical. Hastily however, they thanked the boatman for his insights and quickly carried on with their trek.

Quietly at first, then increasingly hurried, the pair began to pick up the pace, walking faster, then faster as the gloom and anxiety encroached, continuing to envelope them. The light seemed to be fading more rapidly than they anticipated as the shadows of the forest trail grew long and heavy, nipping at their feet. Shade began stretching menacingly across their path. The town still seemed so far away. Would they make it? The conversation diminished, then ceased as their labored breathing overtook their words. Disquiet, foreboding and fear increasingly prodded their steps. Time and the compelling dark pressed them hard. The pangs of panic welled up. Finally unable to contain themselves any further, they broke into a run.

But the jostling of the papers and bundles caused a string to break. No! NO! Not the documents! A roll of irreplaceable sketches and scrolls tumbled to the ground, fanning out as they separated. In their haste to gather them, other bundles toppled in an avalanche of white parchments; reference letters and official credentials. In the breath of a moment the darkened forest fluttered with the white ghosts of important papers, carried by the increasing breeze into its vast depths. Everything scattered about and afar. The pair halted, immediately beginning the laborious task of hunting and gathering the many precious items.

During the scurry to recover them, precious papers and artwork were torn, soiled and wrinkled. Some were never found at all. By the time the remaining items had been gathered back together and secured once again, it was dark. Turning once more toward the village, their fears were confirmed. The path to the town now lay vacant; the gates securely bolted. The long night had begun...the duo's future unknown.

Fear would most likely be named the culprit that caused the pair's undue haste and brought their undoing.

Yet in truth their undoing occurred much earlier in the day when they had heard but decided not to listen. Later in the forest, even as they clung tightly to their bundles and picked up their pace, listening remained a choice they ignored. Electing to have considered the advice of someone experienced could have calmed their steps and safeguarded their arrival.

Imagine how much fear, panic, dilemma and disaster could vanish from our own journey if we undertook an additional moment to slow our pace; choosing to step beyond mere hearing, and truly listen. Providing genuine attention may make the paths we take in life more successful.

7
Sovereign Discernment
10th Century B.C.E.

It had been less than a day since the sumptuous feast recognizing his ascension to the throne around 10th Century B.C.E. The reverberating din in the royal chamber escalated to near unbearable proportions. Certainly the halls of King David, the previous ruler, had never endured such clamor. Here before the splendor of the new monarch, the shrill screaming of obscenities and threats echoed as two dirty, crude prostitutes hissed, slashed and tore at each other.

Protected by their armor, the royal guards sought to separate the wildly clawing women; yet the fervor of the prostitutes' vehemence raged so savagely that the soldiers nervously edged back from the screaming combatants. Between the vicious females and the tense guards cautiously attempting to isolate them lay a wailing infant; the focus of the earsplitting and riotous brawl.

Just beyond the ruckus stood an assemblage of influential international and national dignitaries already set in their positions for presentation to the throne. Attendants from the previous day's coronation feast, they were gathered to formally meet and establish connections with the recently crowned monarch, a youth under 15 years old. Instead their attention now focused upon this untried sovereign, scrutinizing every detail of the situation to determine the weakness, strength, wisdom, and caliber of his leadership and his future as king of Israel.

In recent months, word spread far and wide regarding this teenager and his astounding gift of discernment rumored to have been received from God. Having watched the ebb and flow of his father's reign through triumphs, then tragedies, Solomon recognized the importance of insight. Feeling young and inadequate to rule the kingdom, Solomon had requested the gift of wisdom from God, believing it would enable him to better guide and direct his people. Now within hours of his ordination, Solomon's gift found itself sorely tested.

With venomous accusation, the conflict between the women emerged: Two prostitutes sharing living quarters had both become pregnant. Within three days of the other one, each gave birth to a son. One night one negligent mother rolled over upon her child and smothered it. Despairing, and believing the other woman would not notice, she stealthily placed her dead baby next to her roommate and sequestered the other's living child as her own. Upon rising the next morning to nurse her baby, the roommate suffered the heart-wrenching shock and anguish of the tiny, lifeless body that would have been her son. Recognizing hers as the living child, the mother's pain turned to raging, incendiary fury at the other woman's vehement denials of child stealing. In response, the childless woman spewed scathing, scornful, taunting accusations that the true mother had suffocated her own son to death; punctuating her tirade with bitter, viperous denials and deliberate, defiant declarations that the living child was her own.

The young teen pondered the entire scene before him. This current set of circumstances did not present the kind of royal decision upon which the boy king had hoped to establish the foundation for his reputation and launch his legacy.

Solomon also recognized this problem should not likely have escalated to his level in the first place. According to ancient Jewish custom and law, both of these troublesome prostitutes would have been taken before any number of intermediate adjudicators, juries or religious authorities to have the matter considered. The fact they now embroiled in cat fighting before him for royal judgment could portend more than the problem at hand. A set-up by Solomon's detractors? A means of forcing the inexperienced leader to falter before the visiting dignitaries and his own people? An attempt to destroy his reign before it began? A questionable decision could instigate a palace coup to eliminate him; any new monarch has enemies. Solomon's future and that of his country hung in the balance of this moment.

However amidst this escalating pressure pot of volatile emotions and shrill screaming, the ability for anyone to concentrate soon evaporated like dried grass in a desert flame. It made little difference now how the matter may have arrived at Solomon's feet; it now fell to the youthful king to make the right decision.

Carefully studying the two women, the answer came to him. Perhaps he should not make the decision.

As he held up his hand, the room fell silent. Solomon pointed first to one woman, and then the other as he announced to everyone before him, "This one says, 'THIS is my son who is living, and your son is the DEAD one'; and the other one says, 'NO! For YOUR son is the dead one, and MY son is the living one.' " He continued, "Then to each of these women will be appointed equal custody of the boy."

The teenage sovereign turned to his bodyguard and commanded a sword be brought forward. Immediately one was presented. "Take the sword," he ordered the guard, "Divide the living child in two. Give half to the one and half to the other."

Onlookers gasped in sheer shock and horror. What kind of tyranny…what breed of insanity…what manner of warped wisdom and discernment was this? Somewhere within the shadows of the court attentive minds schemed and sinister smiles curled with anticipation.

One guard stepped forward to separate the child from the women. Collectively the gathering held their breath in a silence so thick it could be sliced with the very sword that the soldier now gripped ominously over the small, frightened, crying child.

Suddenly in an outburst of sheer anguish, one of the prostitutes screamed out. Breaking free from the restraining guards she rushed forward and flung herself prostrate before the feet of King Solomon. Sobbing uncontrollably, she pleaded for his majesty to let the child live, "Give her the living child, and by no means slay him!" The other combative woman, howled with derision. "Divide him! Divide him!! Tear the child asunder and let justice be done!" she jeered. "Let the infant be neither mine nor hers."

Solomon did not hesitate. He arose from his throne. The room's occupants retreated back into an absolute silence. Gesturing toward the woman lying on the floor sobbing, Solomon gave his decree, "Give the living child to the first woman, and by no means kill him. She is his mother." He had recognized the true mother through her willingness to sacrifice deeply for her own child.

Once more gasps surged through the assemblage…but this time of astonishment and admiration, recognizing Solomon did truly possess great wisdom and discernment. The critics were silenced. A timeless reputation ignited and spread like wildfire across the nations of the earth. A legacy for all time began.

But look closely, King Solomon rendered his first and most storied verdict by *not* making the decision. One of the most famous and recognized resolutions in history, the initial verdict for what has been called the reign of the world's wisest man…and the new king of Israel delegated the response to a stranger; the mother of the child.

Solomon sought and received the gift of wisdom and discernment from God. In this case it was the wisdom not to assume his title as king

25

authorized him to know every answer, and the discernment to recognize when the insight of another would present better clarity than his own.

In any role of leadership today, it is a wise lesson to note and use well.

8
A Real Steal
1626 C.E.

Over nearly four centuries it has grown, becoming more deeply embedded with each retelling. A classic tale in American history, the $24.00 in eye-catching baubles, beads and trinkets stands among the first and most enduring records of real estate swindling in United States history; the early acquisition of Manhattan Island.

The popular narrative of the account arose with Mary J. Lamb, writing 259 years after the event in <u>History of the City of New York,</u> 1877. From that point onward, Lamb's view remained firmly entrenched, accepted, taught and unchanged, presenting the Europeans as savvy profiteers, and as carried through U.S. history, the Indians as simpletons. Was she right?

Unlike the imperialist countries building permanent settlements in the New World, the colonial philosophy of the Dutch amounted to a simple credo: Go out. Make lots of money. Go back home to Holland. Live well. Peter Minuet, well-versed in the Dutch entrepreneurial viewpoint, landed in 1626 as newly appointed leader of the Dutch West India Company for the New World. His destination: little more than a paltry collection of meager shanties on the Hudson River. A struggling settlement of employees owned by the Dutch West India Company, it existed solely as a conduit for company commodities shipped to Europe.

The singular interest for Minuet and his employers rested in the area's lucrative fur trade. Valuable pelts funneled to the village from a number of trappers operating along the Hudson River Valley. When Minuet arrived and viewed the tiny, struggling, hardscrabble island outpost now under his management nothing about it remotely hinted that Manhattan Island could someday grow into the center of the world-renowned metropolis, New York City.

Looking to curry his status with the company, Peter soon determined that this location at the mouth of the Hudson River and flanked by the Atlantic Ocean commanded strategic views of the region. The possibility to commercially and militarily dominate areas up the river with its deep inland tributaries caught his attention. Recognizing the island's potential to develop and centralize shipping trade, Peter Minuit decided the purchase of the island for the Dutch West India Company would be a good business decision and potential feather in his cap.

Minuet quickly had the word spread to various indigenous peoples of the area that he wished to legally buy the island. In due course, emerging one misty morning from across the river, a contingency of Canarsie Indians arrived by canoes to the island. Presenting themselves officially and seeking to transact business, they eventually struck a deal with Minuit.

The Canarsie were sharp negotiators. They did not negotiate for trinkets. Knowing the Europeans eagerly sought the island, the natives understood they held the advantage. The tribe proceeded to inquire about the village and its contents. Then they scrutinized, haggled and bartered for items of exceptional value, items they could see the villagers highly prized. The Indians collected a treasure trove of significant equipment: heavy iron kettles, sharpened steel axe heads, cultivating hoes, drilling awls of various sizes, lengths of rugged duffel cloth and other diverse wares. Along with the array of settler's crucial tools, the Indians also requested cherished items including the costly Venetian and Dutch glass beads, highly esteemed throughout Europe and particularly dear to the colonists. Even the few, treasured mouth harps, the colonists' limited means of music were relinquished.

For the Dutch company workers, most of them indentured servants, these items ranked no small sacrifice. In the century prior to the 1750's Industrial Revolution, every item, no matter how simple or who it was for, demanded individual handcrafting. Skilled and even not so skilled artisans in Europe that had apprenticed for their trade would command premium prices for their products. This meant that items purchased were not only precious and treated well, but often handed down through generations. The value propounded as pioneers coming to the New World on small ships could pack only the bare essentials. Everything and anything they were allowed to bring with them was vital; carefully and thoughtfully selected, paid for dearly to transit, and once here, treasured. It could not be replaced in the new land. Space for personal items or family reminders was not an option. Still a mouth harp or a few beautiful Dutch-made glass beads were slipped into some pockets to remind the company colonists of home until they could return.

Beyond being worth their weight in gold, the tools and pots provided the settlers' survival. This irreplaceable equipment served the ability to build shelters, to clear land and cultivate it for food, to obtain firewood for cooking and winter warmth. The Indians quickly comprehended that these implements enabled a far more fruitful existence than the tribe currently fared.

By the afternoon, the colonists surveyed the spoils assembled by the Canarsie. No baubles used as payment here. The Canarsie drove a very hard bargain. In the end Minuet agreed to the barter and required his business owned colony to surrender a goodly portion of their prized possessions in order to secure ownership of the island for the Dutch West Indies Company.

The documents were notated. The compensation exchanged hands. The villagers watched with mixed emotion as their precious personal articles were summarily gathered into blankets by the strangers and unceremoniously dragged down to the shore. With canoes now heavily laden with loot, the Indians pushed their wobbling boats off the shore and into the water. The Canarsie then happily rowed up the Hudson River slowly vanishing into the afternoon shafts of fading sunlight, their boats precariously pitching just above the waterline. While his constituents may have held second thoughts, Peter Minuet, quite pleased, congratulated himself on his shrewd trade.

And truly, a cunning transaction was concluded.

From the Dutch workers' perspective, the deal soured quickly. The desolate island where the settler's had already struggled greatly to survive now attacked their severely limited resources with a vengeance. Brutal weather patterns increased, bringing strong cold winds that swept the area producing wretched, unrelenting winters. The sweltering summers brought swarms of invading insects and widespread disease. Manhattan proved so inhospitable that Minuit soon uprooted and relocated the colony to the other side of the island, hoping the scrub forests might mitigate the miserable conditions and the endless sea of swamps. So heartening to know the company owned the island now…

On the other hand, having rowed away with new tools of civilization they could never have imagined in their traditional lives as nomadic Indians, the Canarsie Indians propelled themselves into a better existence.

The Dutch bought dismal swampland and in return the Indians received rare commodities that enriched them beyond mere wealth. There was one other small element that escaped the Dutch. Remember the

Canarsie Tribe got in their boats and paddled away? They actually hailed from the island of Brooklyn. The Weckquasegeek tribe resided seasonally on Manhattan. The clever Canarsie sold the Dutch an island that their tribe didn't live on and that didn't belong to them.

Historic lore evolving over the following 250 years painted a far different story, a tale altered by bias. Mary Lamb's book coincided with prevailing media of the day; Remington's vivid, violent portraits of the Plains Indians in Eastern magazines, popular dime novels with lurid narratives of men and women against the savage Indians. The shocking newspaper accounts of the Indian wars, including Custer's Last Stand in 1876, and General Sherman's motto, "The only good Indian is a dead Indian", all reinforced the current prejudice against the Indian people.

Additional investigation completely inverts the common, time-honored perception of the Manhattan real estate deal. Ironically even with the Indians coming out ahead, the story remains the most noted real estate transaction in American history and a classic tale of swindling… but from a different perspective.

In this overwhelmingly fast paced, text messaged, sound-bite driven, narrow focus, and tight camera-angle world, one finds it increasingly easy, and is strongly lobbied to blindly accept information at face value.

A bit of added fact-finding can create a wider perspective in how we think.

9
On a Roll
51 B.C.E.

The immediate future seemed exceptionally bleak for the beautiful 19 year-old princess. The year was 51 B.C.E. Her tradition-bound father had just passed away and following customs set forth since time immemorial, the royal blood had to be kept in the family. This meant that she had to marry the new king…her eleven-year-old kid brother. A repulsive and malicious child, he had learned from his father the art of subtle torture to maintain power, and the practice of quiet murder involving troublesome family members. Depending on how she toed the line, life for the princess now unfolded as either miserably long or painfully short. Either way it appeared pretty much over for her.

Concurrently there emerged a greater problem. A far-away, massive empire intent on expansion even now marched an unstoppable army of conquest toward the old kingdom.

What's a lovely teenage princess to do?

Weighing the situation, she surmised that her best chance of survival on her own terms lay in teaming with the opposition. Her status as royalty and her knowledge on every aspect of the kingdom might be bartered for a position of stature if she assisted the invaders. At least she might endure longer… and she could escape her vicious little brother.

The problem confronting her consisted of somehow getting through a maze of royal soldiers and security. How could she escape the palace and its guards? Then comes the really tough part: How does one penetrate the minion of hostile forces to gain an audience with the commanding general of this enemy? She had heard he was a man of great distinction, taste, leadership and class. Certainly he would be surrounded by layers of bureaucracy: officers, personal guards and a retinue.

She paced the floor intently racking her brain for an idea. There seemed no way to accomplish her plan. She thought and thought about the best way to approach this distinguished leader to get a personal message to him. Finally, she glanced down. The answer lay right before her; right at her feet. She would stake her future on a roll of carpeting…

A short time later the invading General sat in his headquarters, conducting the business of conquest. His servants suddenly approached saying that a precious gift had arrived from the old royal family of the ancient kingdom currently slated for imminent occupation. It was a roll of carpet. Having heard that the country of origin possessed a distinguished reputation for its fine weavings and textiles, the General ordered it be brought before him at once, anxious to see what exquisite treasure might be unfurled before him.

The kingdom's emissaries lay down the massive carpet, unrolled it and everyone gasped in delight at the treasure the carpet held…the princess herself! She had had her servants roll her within the rug. It managed not only to get her past the palace guards at home, but got her through the invading army and right to the feet of their commander.

And thus in 51 B.C.E., Julius Caesar gained introduction to the legendary innovation and beguiling charms of the lovely teenage Egyptian princess known as Cleopatra. Her cleverness would eventually cull the favor of two Roman leaders. With Julius Caesar she brokered a situation to allow her kingdom to be an independent ally of Rome and not be absorbed as a puppet state. For herself, Cleopatra of course arranged to be Queen of Egypt, and she attained an immortal station in the annals of history. Her brother finds no further mention of importance in the annals. Apparently she took care of him too.

So often we become wrapped in our fretting and worries, visualizing only the problems that are to come, overlooking possible solutions. Sometimes the keys to success lay right at our feet. All that might be required is to roll up ourselves in a bit of innovation, imagination, boldness and determination.

Seek to develop and follow through on those traits
…and perhaps end up becoming legendary.

10
Sign of a Foothold
July 1907 C.E.

At the turn of the 20th Century seemingly the most joyous place to be on the face of the earth could be found on a few acres south of New York City surmounted by a cheerful, smiling face overwhelmed by its broad, toothy grin.

Steeplechase Park as the place was named, literally brimmed; crammed with rides, people, food concessions and games. This Coney Island landmark tantalized, offering the forbidden of Victorian society: uninhibited interaction and touchably-close proximity. The enclave found immediate and lasting popularity, particularly among young people sneaking the frowned upon intimacy among dark rides, coasters and the huge, pressing crowds. Encircling Steeplechase Park and arbitrating entry into its mystique lay the steeplechase ride itself. On parallel tracks a series of double-saddle wooden horses raced along an undulating trail with the more weighted horse generally winning. Since boys frequently made bets on the outcome, "big-boned" girls found high popularity, a squeezably close encounter on the careening horses and a probable date for the evening by frequenting the Steeplechase ride.

Steeplechase blossomed for a solid decade from 1897 until the day the luck ran out in 1907. Amusement parks of the era always faced a huge gamble. Their facades consisted of little more than boards covered with hemp, plaster and paint. They burned easily, quickly and usually without the benefit of insurance.

On a fateful July day in 1907, the dream and the joy were obliterated. The eighteen hour fire that consumed Steeplechase spread rapidly and burned furiously. It felled the massive roller coasters, the ornate towers and gaudy buildings. Roaring hot and high, contrasting a brilliant red into the darkened, soot filled skies, the conflagration could be seen for miles. The fire burned throughout the evening. Nothing, absolutely nothing had been spared. Huge crowds came out, standing through the night and into the wee morning hours, watching the inferno rise and fall inside the high walls surrounding the park. They sighed and screamed in fright and dismay as one by one the popular rides and structures became immersed in flame, then strained in loud death knells as steel and wood failed, and finally crumpled in showers of sparks, flames and flashes.

George Tilyou, the Steeplechase owner and a master promoter of Coney Island dating back to his teen years, arrived early the next morning. Sidling through the massive crowd of sympathizers and curious onlookers, he quietly sauntered into the park privately and surveyed the debris of his rides, concessions and livelihood. Blackened piles of rubble and ruin, smoldering and smoking wreckage appeared all that remained. Some scattered fires still leapt and crackled, almost appearing to gloat and mock Tilyou even as the weary firemen sought to finally extinguish them. Everything was gone. With all before him a total loss, uninsured and thus without recompense to even begin again, the nearly 50 year-old Tilyou had every reason and right to sink to the depths of depression. Yet Tilyou knew that even disaster can carry the earmarks of possibility.

Thinking quickly, he immediately ordered a sign painted and promptly planted outside the still standing walls of his devastated Steeplechase Park. The posted notice proclaimed that Tilyou remained undaunted and optimistic, promising to build a better and even grander park on that exact same spot.

…and knowing human nature, he requested the bottom of the sign to read prominently:

"Admission to burning ruins 10 cents."

The crowds lined up for days.

No matter the calamity or devastation, no matter what the disaster, there always exists a foothold…a place to take that next step forward. No matter where we find ourselves, we should look for that foothold and take that step.

Footholds take unusual shapes. George Tilyou's foothold after the fire, a simple sign, re-affirmed his belief in himself and his abilities. The park was soon rebuilt. The huge, smiling face proclaiming Steeplechase Park beamed once more. Perhaps this time it was not so much a grin of mirth as it was the smile of confidence.

In the aftermath of flame and ash, in the rubble and ruin of life's plans:

  …ascertain your possibilities
  …find that foothold
  …paint the sign.

34

11
14 Cows
June 2002 C.E.

Around an island of light the impenetrable black of the night halts and lingers, dodging and dancing with occasional intrusion at the ragged edge of a confidently robust, crackling bonfire. In a tradition dating from time immemorial, communication of news travels in customary fashion; sharing amongst tribesmen who sit at night around a bright, roaring blaze. Many times in this very remote speck on the map, news can take time to arrive.

Enoosaen, tucked far, far away in the deep, trackless savannah of Africa, exists as a place outside of time; a hamlet constituting a collection of small mud and thatch huts on dirt. This remote Kenyan village of earthen huts near the Tanzanian border is home to the proud Maasai, one of the most isolated and most traditional of tribes. The only paved road is a 100-yard stretch of tarmac about fifteen rugged, dirt miles away. Two and a half hours of rough road afield of that the Masai Mara Wildlife preserve spreads out. Another three hours hard driving beyond that one finally finds the city of Nairobi.

On this night in this faraway place seemingly at the end of the earth, the solemn men gazed intently into the bright, dancing flames and listened spellbound as one of their own shared a terrifying, yet compelling tale of horror in a distant realm; a story beyond their greatest imaginations. Wilson Kimeli Naiyomah, a young man returning from studying abroad related his gripping eyewitness tale of a huge city with great buildings rising into the heavens. The two highest towers, the ones reaching deepest into the clouds were attacked by evil enemies. The twin buildings burned so furiously that the smoke could be seen from outer space. People leapt from the windows to their death. Then the structures collapsed with thunderous roars, hurling storming clouds of wreckage everywhere. The rescuers and many more people ensnared within the towers died when the buildings fell from the sky.

This dumbfounded the tribesmen living on the African savannah where the tallest things to see were giraffes and scrub trees. The report seemed afar of belief since the tribal huts are not even six feet tall and falling from the highest scrub tree might merely bruise a man. The natives struggled to visualize the idea of falling to one's death. But they understood death. And the death of nearly 3,000 innocent people, equal to the population in Enoosaen, through four coordinated attacks by purely evil men brought forth just anger in these tribal leaders.

The Maasai elders may not have grasped parts of the event told, but they clearly comprehended the heart of the matter: A great people and generous friend had been brutally attacked by the same malevolent Al-Qaeda that had three years earlier coordinated bombings in Tanzania and Nairobi, killing hundreds of native Kenyans. With recent memories of their own loss still fresh, Wilson and the elders listening by the fire that night later related that the horrific attack on America brought anguish and tears to even the strongest of the tribesmen. The Maasai, considered ferocious warriors, felt a fierce frustration at not being there to help their friends in this time of desperate need. While fearless, they are a people with a genuine heart and open compassion for those they care about deeply.

Angered and wanting to do something, the Maasai determined that they must come to the aid of their ally. Their numbers were small yet many would have willingly gone forward. But the village could not afford to part with their best warriors to fight far away for their friends. The tribal leaders discussed the matter. Unable to contribute and support a fighting force, what could they do?

A gift of cows arose as the unanimous answer.

The Maasai culture and people have remained relatively unchanged in this desolate region for thousands of years. Known as the "people of cattle" they carry forward their proud and ageless tradition as bush warriors and cow caretakers. Until recently young boys needed to fearlessly confront a lion or other large predator in the wild and spear it to death before finding acceptance as a man. From childhood, they learn that the greatest dignity in life is defending the cattle. As men they will courageously put their lives on the line to fight off lions, leopards and other predators of the village's lifeblood, the herd.

The sun-scorched and parched land of Eastern Africa rebuffs attempts at crops and agriculture. Life in its totality remains tied to the relationship with the herd. The very survival of the Maasai people in this impoverished area depends upon the health and strength of their herds and their beloved cattle. Cattle are the payment, the debt, the loan, and purpose in the tribe. To a family, ownership of even a single cow signifies one's wealth, prestige, and status.

In appreciation to the Zebu cattle for their role toward Enoosaen's survival, the Maasai bond emotionally with them. Culture, social relations, ritual, ceremonial life, symbolism, even idioms of language relate to their devotion of the cattle. The single cow or multiples that belong to a family are children to them. Should one die, each part of the animal finds honored use; horns for containers, hooves and bones as fashion ornaments, and hides cured for shoes, clothing, blankets and ropes. In inclement weather treasured animals are brought into the hut. Every animal possesses a distinctive voice and temperament well-known to their family. Young calves are tenderly cared for and fussed over as though they were newborn children. Zebu cows and bulls are included in all religious and spiritual observances. Songs are sung that express affection for their beloved bovines.

From generations immemorial life has been and continues to be intrinsically linked to cattle. From one's birth to the grave, cows dominate every aspect of life. In childbirth, celebration, marriage and sympathy for the grieving, cows reign a central point for tribal culture, ceremony, economy, existence and purpose...supremely valued; the ultimate gift.

"We saw the Americans in pain, we asked what we could give to express our sorrow, something that was so central to us, and that was the cows." explained their tribal leader, "They are the handkerchiefs we Maasai use to wipe away tears."

The tribe had decided. They would give the greatest gift the tribe ever assembled.

"They give what is truly sacred to them." explains Naiyomah. "There are three most cherished things that a Maasai can offer as a gift -- a child, a plot of land and a cow. "The cow is almost the center of life for us. It is sacred. It is more than property. You give it a name. You talk to it. You perform rituals with it. This is the ultimate gift a Maasai can give."

And so on June 3rd, 2002, by the special request of this little village at the edge of the earth, the acting United States Ambassador to Kenya, William Brencick arrived in the hamlet to accept a great honor. The Maasai formally and solemnly presented the Ambassador with their supreme gift of 14 cows. Precious livestock presented to help the United States heal from the suffering caused by the September 11th, 2001 attack on the World Trade Center in New York City, the Pentagon in Washington DC and Flight 93 in Pennsylvania.

Some in the modern world laughed, deriding the Maasai as a backwards people for offering such impractical and useless aid. What could the United States possibly do with 14 scrawny cows stuck in the wilds of a continent half a planet away? Transporting them would cost a fortune. Customs issues, climate changes, diseases carried...what were they thinking? Even the price they might fetch in the nearest big African city would likely not bring a pittance to the U. S. Obviously these villagers couldn't begin to comprehend the magnitude of 9/11 nor fathom the affluence of the United States. However, people in the modern world can be blinded by preconceptions and prejudices. Veils of sophistication can prevent us from seeing the heart of the matter.

The African natives saw everything with profound clarity. To a friend in great need the Maasai people, deemed among the world's most meager in worldly possessions and resources, bestowed the largest offering ever gathered of their precious cattle.

No biased opinions or prejudice blinded the Maasai. They did not permit perceptions of astonishing wealth, innumerable possessions, unimaginable technology or massive distance to deter them from their desire to respond. The Maasai chose to look beyond small-mindedness, focusing on the heart of the matter. They chose only to view people hurting and in grief. As a people, the Maasai exhibited the very best of humanity in their genuineness and in their great personal sacrifice.

When will we look past our prejudices and perceptions, recognizing the heart of the matter with clarity, and prompting a sacrifice of the fullest measure?

Our own equivalent of 14 cows.

12
Better Than His Word
December, 1843 C.E.

It is probably the second most well known holiday story ever written. The tale emerged an instant and immense, popular phenomenon from the day it was first published on December 19, 1843. With no publicity, the initial six thousand copies sold out in five days. From then until now it has never been out of print. Penned by a debt-strapped British author, the narrative vividly recalled many English rituals that had faded into disuse and abandonment. The story resulted in an immediate resurgence of these customs that are still held dear even to the present. In over 160 years of retelling, the tale moved beyond popular, entering into beloved tradition.

In all probability, the reader of this piece may have never actually read this renowned book, yet you know it by heart. How could one sum up something so thoroughly that they may never have read? The answer is that we are steeped in its traditions, enchanted by its hauntings. Chances are good that if only one key word of the book's text were printed here, the reader would be able to name at least five major characters and tell the entire story, scene by scene. One could easily give details about the various interactions, character costumes and locations, and even quote some of the dialogue. It is THAT well known.

The strange issue though arises from the fact that although we collectively know this tome by heart, very few know the moral of the tale. It has been lost in our love of ...well, badness. In all seriousness, our society has developed a deep interest in villains. We revel in the revile. In the case of this story, we love to hate the bad guy so much that his despicable character has grown to become a hallmark we enjoy, anticipate and even relish with each telling of the piece.

And that is why the true meaning of the tale has been largely lost. While the missing moral arrives, routinely recited with each retelling, it appears as a side bar to the primary richness of the prime character's vile nature, a cantankerous demeanor that seems to offer so much odd pleasure to us.

Is anyone still uncertain of the story? With one word, the entire tale will leap into the collective consciousness, providing all the details

previously mentioned that the reader would recall. Ready? Here we
go…

　　　Scrooge…

　　　So, all those light bulbs switched on quickly, didn't they?
Suddenly Charles Dickens' <u>A Christmas Carol</u> leaps to full life in your
mind. From Ebenezer Scrooge's initial "Bah! Humbug!" to Tiny Tim's
gentle nature. Jacob Marley's Ghost came forth with his unforgettable
baggage of cashboxes, books and ledgers chained to him; returning as a
faithful friend to offer Scrooge the chance for hope and redemption. The
Spirit of Christmas' Past, Present and Yet-To-Come sail through memory.
A host of memorable characters from Bob Crachit to Mr. Fezziwig march
and dance through your thoughts. Scrooge's counting house, Ebenezer's
bed chamber, Bob's house, the cemetery and much more drift and shift as
the scenes retell the narrative. This story wove the cloth for many of our
Christmas customs and ingrained within collective memory the entire
concept of a Victorian themed Christmas.

　　　What follows is a condensation of the final paragraph in the book.
As one continues to read, it will reveal itself plainly that the way we
perceive this timeless tale subtly subjugates the real moral to the story.
Indeed, we have overlooked the very best and richest lesson.

　　　*"Scrooge was better than his word. He did it all, and infinitely
more; and to Tiny Tim, who did not die, he was a second father. He
became as good a friend, as good a master, and as good a man, as the
good old city knew, or any other good old city, town, or borough, in the
good old world…*

　　　*…and it was always said of him, that he knew how to keep
Christmas well, if any man alive possessed the knowledge. May that be
truly said of us, and all of us!*

　　　Instead of an angry, dour old miser, there should be a recollection
of a person who gained hope; a changed man who would celebrate the
season throughout the remaining years and days in his life so joyously
that he himself became a joyous celebration to all he came in contact.

　　　*"I will honor Christmas in my heart, and try to keep it all the
year."*

That was Scrooge's quintain. That is what the book says, indeed, the moral of the tale…a person that in the end strove to be better than his word, and as good a friend as can be found.

Being just like Ebenezer Scrooge…
May that be truly said of us, and all of us!

13
Power of Presumption
December, 1937 C.E.

On this particularly cold and snowy night of December 19th, 1937, in Nanjing, China, a half dozen heavily armed Japanese soldiers scaled the tall wall of the private estate and dropped into the garden of the foreign emissary's home. They moved with a sense of invincibility. There appeared scant concern that anyone in the compound might hear them. Their purpose: pure evil. Their objective: break the locks on the iron entry gates and unleash a horde of bloodthirsty comrades into the walled compound. Their goal: slaughter the Chinese refugees sequestered behind the walls. Simple killing loomed far from their intent. The soldiers had earlier calculated countless horrendous tortures to enact, vicious brutal rapes to inflict, cold blooded executions to mete out, and rampant butchery to exact.

Soon after the Japanese reached the gates and set to bashing the lock, a weak flashlight beam caught their attention. An unassuming, older, bespectacled European man shining a flashlight at them had interrupted their progress. Bald with a pasty complexion, wearing a trim little moustache barely as wide as his nose, his appearance was that of a milquetoast character who might be found sitting behind a desk each day, shuffling papers.

With malevolent intent, the soldiers closest to the disrupter drew pistols, aiming to kill him on the spot. The intended target glared, then began raging at them with an indignant, commanding voice. He pulled out an armband emblazoned with his country's flag and waved it in their faces, demanding they respect him, the sovereignty of his position and that they immediately withdraw the way they arrived…climbing back over the fence. The Japanese soldiers hesitated, glowered at him, then reluctantly holstered their weapons and soon retreated over the same wall they first climbed. The gathering of Chinese refugees tucked away in the estate grounds, living on tattered straw mats, abandoned old doors, and scavenged sheets of tin providing little protection from the snow and winter cold were grateful…all 600 of them.

Far from an isolated incident, this intense game of life and death occurred in Nanjing daily. Yet somehow John Rabe continued to find the bravery to stand against one of the greatest horrors of modern history and the depraved savagery as it unfolded around him.

Several years prior to that December night in 1937, Japan's military high command had deemed it their destiny to rule a Global Empire. By 1932, their expansionist strategies ignited what would become the Sino-Japanese war. Sino *(China),* a country weakened by a collapsing central government and a civil war raging between Nationalist and Communist factions, could offer little resistance to Japan's formidable invading army. From the start, the Japanese military quickly seized advantage over their huge mainland neighbor. Having stormed the southern provinces, the merciless and unrelenting conquering army next invaded China's northern provinces by sea in 1937; rampaging through the major port city of Shanghai then piercing deep into the country's central region. The now defeated and disarrayed splinters of Chinese militia had retreated to the hinterlands. Continuing to press inland, the invading Japanese Empire's path of Chinese eradication pointed directly to the ancient Chinese capital, Nanjing.

On November 22, 1937, the day before his 55th birthday, events unleashed that changed the lives of John Rabe and the 1.5 million Chinese residents of Nanjing. Mass destruction and annihilation does not require fleets of planes and stockpiles of bombs. It can be accomplished by groups of ordinary soldiers...it just takes a little longer.

A plain-looking, bespectacled, unobtrusive fellow, Rabe displayed few earmarks of great leadership. In China for 27 years, he had worked quietly for Siemens, a global electronics firm, rising to become their senior representative brokering major deals with the Chinese government for electronics, telephones and motors. His cultural knowledge and contacts had also earned him appointment as his nation's ambassador to the Chinese government.

As the Japanese army advanced on Nanjing, Rabe determined not to evacuate when nearly 800,000 others did. He instead remained behind with a few dozen other foreign nationals, mostly missionaries, scholars and doctors. This small coterie quickly planned out a temporary "International Safe Zone" for the Nanjing foreign residents from neutral countries.

A 15-member committee of international residents was elected to administer the International Safe Zone with Rabe selected as leader. This safe haven of protected properties in the western district of the city consisted primarily of foreign embassies, the University of Nanjing, several private estates and twenty-five hostels encompassing an area measuring around seven square kilometers or about six square miles.

Unarmed and unassuming, hoping against hope they would not be mowed down on the spot in a hail of bullets, Rabe and his small group walked out and met the invading Japanese military. The little group of dignitaries explained to the advancing army hierarchy of their diplomatic status and the neutrality of the International Safe Zone they had established. Their ruse, accepted for the moment, enabled tens of thousands of Chinese refugees to quickly flood the safe zone, primarily those unable to evacuate yet desperately seeking survival.

Rabe and the committee members had no idea how long they could keep the invaders from simply killing them and annihilating their refugees. But for now the ploy to protect what Chinese they could, worked…at least within the zone. The rest of the region proved a different and gruesome story.

Later branded "The Rape of Nanjing", the remainder of the city suffered through six grisly weeks of unrelenting slaughter and abominable destruction during the Japanese army's occupation. Japanese troops wildly looted and torched Nanjing and the surrounding towns. One third of the ancient capital of China was burned to the ground. Tens of thousands of Chinese civilians and surrendering Chinese soldiers died horribly. Chinese captives were tortured, decapitated, burnt alive, plowed over by tanks after being buried to their necks, used for bayonet practice and shot en masse by the thousands. Eighty thousand Chinese women and girls of all ages were brutally raped and thousands then murdered after their ordeal. Others ended up forced into sexual slavery as "Comfort Women" for the soldiers until they died from the abuse. These six weeks are generally considered the worst single massacre of unarmed troops and civilians in the history of the 20th Century.

In the center of this incredible carnage stood John Rabe, an unassuming, unarmed fellow who guarded the International Safe Zone from the marauding Japanese army. Rabe also opened his personal estate to shelter 600 refugees. He remained diligent, keeping at bay the constantly prowling Japanese. Rabe simply hoped his bluff held out as the screams, gunfire and grisly visions of death throughout the rest of the city crept constantly closer.

Daily he used his presence, influence and ambassador credentials to halt whatever violence he could. To chronicle the event, John compiled a 1,200 page diary of the experiences and the horror. By his own admission, he almost could not bear the ever increasing masses of mutilated corpses; the continuous violent deaths at a staggering toll of over 7,000 Chinese people per day.

After six weeks of utter carnage, the Japanese army marched relentlessly onward to further conquests. 300,000 innocent lives in Nanjing were deemed lost, yet in the end, a quarter of a million people survived sheltered in the 52 buildings and compounds provided by the International Safe Zone and a handful of people led by John Rabe.

The prominent red armband that John Rabe proudly and constantly wore; the one he had used that December night to send the soldiers scrambling away, was emblazoned with a black swastika in a white circle. John Rabe was a loyal Nazi and ardent admirer of Adolf Hitler. Due to his protected political situation as German ambassador, his invoking of Hitler and Germany demanded and commanded respect with the Japanese military, since they had military treaties with the Nazis. This ordinary, unarmed man survived against an army of annihilation and conquest and saved the lives of nearly 250,000 Chinese.

To this day he is a hero in China.
They see past the symbols in his life and the color of his skin.
They do not see the armband…only the man.

It would behoove us to view people by content of character rather than by symbols displayed or the color of skin.

When it comes to others, how do we see?

14
Silently Speaking Volumes
1969 C.E.

In the late 1960's, early 1970's many American youth immersed themselves in the growing hippie movement. Adorned with long hair, eclectic clothing and unconventional lifestyle, these young people rejected the mores of established society, their parents' aspirations, and the traditional values in life. Through vast, high profile protests and gatherings including speeches, chanting and singing, they preached peace and love, no war, anti-establishment, non-violence, sexual promiscuity and drug experimentation. Massive "Love-Ins" and the battle cry of "Sex, Drugs, and Rock & Roll" frustrated parent/child relationships, fragmented society and swept the wild imagination of an impressionable generation. Although national in scope, the flash point for this counter-culture developed in Northern California, radiating its message and example to the rest of the nation from the Haight-Ashbury district of San Francisco.

During those tumultuous times, another movement had quietly begun growth in Southern California. Its adherents looked like the hippies: longhaired, unkempt young people congregating in parks, beaches and similar, large, public places. These flower children also sat about in festival style, singing folk songs while discussing peace and revolution. Notably though, the sex and drugs were missing. In their place was a single element...Jesus Christ.

Widely radiating from Southern California, the "Jesus People" movement can be largely attributed to one man...a quiet, friendly fellow who pastored a small church in Costa Mesa called Calvary Chapel. Beginning in the late 1960's, these young, hippie-like Jesus People, carrying their well-worn Bibles and songbooks, began flocking to this little country church. Throughout the 1970's, the small church kept growing. Nightly, attendees numbering in the thousands regularly overflowed the three-ring circus tent used while the new larger sanctuary was being built. The pastor's secret, as he told it, derived from the fact that he simply gave out the unchanging and uncompromised word of God directly from the Bible. He taught simply and straightforward...verse by verse, chapter by chapter, book by book.

But that wasn't all that he did.

Consider one example:

About 1969, the conventional, somewhat staid congregation decided to upgrade the small, original church. They installed a beautiful blue, wall-to-wall carpet across the sanctuary. Soon afterwards the elders came to Pastor Smith and complained to him that the hippie youth attending the church in increasing numbers were usually barefoot and their feet, filthy. The habits of these newcomers would quickly soil the new carpet. It was suggested that they be turned away and told to come back after they cleaned themselves up or bought shoes. Something had to be done about them. They must learn respect for the church.

Pastor Chuck carefully considered the elders' concerns and calmly agreed that the expensive new carpet should be protected. And yes, something would have to be done about the barefoot hippies tracking in dirt. And yes, everyone should learn respect. He told them he would have a solution by the following Sunday.

The next Sunday the hippies arrived, barefoot and dirty. But this Sunday they were met individually at the door of the church by the courteous and smiling Pastor Chuck.

With a towel on his shoulder and a bucket of water nearby, Pastor Chuck quietly, and personally, took the time to wash the feet of each and every barefoot hippie who arrived to attend church that day. There came a great silence over everyone that spoke volumes.

The complaints ceased. The flower children began to improve their hygiene. The carpet remained clean. Everyone gained immense respect for the pastor. But most of all, everyone benefited from the opportunity to see the power of Biblical teaching in real life in a most practical sense.

Today there are far beyond 1000 affiliated Calvary Chapel churches across the United States and in many foreign countries. Their worship services are not uncommon to exceed several thousand people.

Does one need to ask how a man of such quiet humbleness without the use of big-time showmanship and controlling leadership skills, manage to enable and impact this movement?

The positive actions that silently speak volumes can enable successful solutions to problems far more effectively than cajoling or criticism.

15
The Merchant of Death
1888 C.E.

On this particular day in 1888 after visiting one of his French factories, Alfred Nobel slumped heavily into an armchair and slowly opened the Paris newspaper. Turning to the back pages, he searched the obituaries for solace and comfort.

Even though one of the world's wealthiest men owing to his invention of dynamite, Nobel felt overwhelming melancholy. First his brother Emil had perished in an 1866 laboratory explosion, then his brother Robert died in 1886. Now in 1888 his last family relation, younger brother Ludvig, had passed away. Ludvig Nobel had risen to become a well respected businessman in Russia, not only for his technical inventions and industrial enterprise, but also for his compassion and rapport with his employees. Ludvig had introduced profit sharing and had strived actively to improve working conditions in his ship building and oil refining factories.

Obviously such a man would be praised and respected by all. In his sadness, Alfred sought the obituary for relief; seeking the reassuring words of admiration regarding his brother that might ease the pain of loss.

But when Alfred's gaze fell upon the death listings, he froze with shock and disquiet. Ludvig's obituary was not listed in the newspaper. It was Alfred's own name, face and story reproduced on the page.

Alfred had dubbed it "dynamite". At the young age of 31 in 1866, Alfred Nobel emerged an instant self-made millionaire with his invention of trinitrotoluene, more familiarly known by the initials TNT. In the years that followed he ascended to become a savvy industrialist of global magnitude and one of the world's richest men,

However the stunning success did not come without severe personal cost. Two years prior to his final achievement in creating his renowned explosive, his brother Emil and several of Alfred's close compatriots had been blown to bits in a huge laboratory blast.

Dynamite's base ingredient, nitroglycerin, is one of the most powerful, unstable explosives ever created. Even a mild shock to a small amount can cause detonation generating massive destruction. In 1867, unwary clerks in a downtown San Francisco parcel delivery storeroom opened a leaky package to check its contents, not realizing the box contained a small vial of nitroglycerin. The resulting blast absolutely pulverized everything within a 50-foot-radius. The heavy brick walls of the bank building withheld much of the extensive damage of the blast that would have leveled the entire block of wood frame structures. Still, for a half mile in every direction windows were blown from structures and body parts of the unfortunate workers had exploded through the roof, scattered atop distant third story apartments. In other words there were never small accidents with nitroglycerin, only horrendous, damaging explosions.

Nevertheless Nobel's harnessing of nitroglycerin's incredible power into a somewhat stable and usable form for TNT, proved revolutionary. Even so many cities and provinces banned his invention, his factories, and occasionally Alfred himself from their borders to avoid the not so uncommon tragedies associated with the production of dynamite.

Although he had been devastated by the shocking loss of Emil in 1866, Alfred pressed onward with his invention. Unending demands from both military and civilian industries for dynamite quickly materialized and Alfred constructed factories that worked around the clock to fulfill the requests. Even with safeguards in place, the factories still suffered explosions with tremendous destruction and loss of life. Yet Nobel's business continued to expand. Nobel built major factories in 20 countries, a substantial accomplishment in an era prior to air travel, automobiles, common electricity or telephones.

It is no small consequence the tremendous progress and pace of construction throughout the world over the next century owed its magnitude to Nobel's invention. Building industries, railroads, roadways, tunnels, bridges, dams, shipping canals, and other major projects worldwide were aided by TNT, and in Nobel's mind, improving mankind's lot.

Nobel believed in the dynamite's potential as a peacemaker. As early as 1876, he had publicly stated his desire to create a material or machine which would have such a devastating effect that war from that point on would be impossible. Years later he stated that "Perhaps my factories will put an end to war sooner than your congresses: on the day that two army corps can mutually annihilate each other in a second, all civilized nations will surely recoil with horror and disband their troops."

Now however, Alfred sat numb and stunned as he began to read. The French newspaper mistook the death of a person named "Nobel" to be the more prominent Alfred currently living in France, not the quiet Ludvig in distant Russia. And like newspapers treat the famous and notable today, they had liberally splashed their opinion of the "late" Alfred Nobel across the pages.

Nobel considered his invention and manufacture of TNT as a gift benefiting humankind. The French press viewed TNT and its inventor far differently. Initially presented as a brilliant chemist, the memorial then bid him good riddance, launching into contempt and scorn for Alfred's creation of dynamite and its devastation. "The Merchant of Death is Dead." The paper derided Nobel as a bellicose monster, charging he had earned his fortune in blood money by providing new ways of killing and mutilating. They decried him for boosting the bloody art of war from bullets and bayonets to long-range explosives, thus gaining his riches by enabling people to maim and slaughter to a greater extent. "Only to be remembered for his destructive contribution of TNT, an explosive responsible for many deaths..." the obituary continued to revile Nobel, portraying him as the Dynamite King, the malevolent scientist that had heaped death, destruction and carnage upon humanity.

Being derided and scorned for ones' life work would leave any person bitter. Many would have sued and demanded retraction. But Alfred Nobel recognized he had received a tremendous gift: the opportunity to read his own obituary and learn how the world would regard and speak of him following his death. Nobel saw his legacy...and decided he didn't like it one bit. He determined this gift he had been given would not be lost in anger, self pity or melancholy. He set his mind to alter those glaring and disparaging words before him.

Over the next few years he quietly reflected and prior to his death in 1896, Alfred committed to paper a hand written, one page Last Will and Testament, cramming the margins with details and notes. His final wish encompassed having his entire, massive, international, industrial empire liquidated. Furthermore Alfred ordered the immense profits from this sale to be placed into a fund. And the bank interest from this fund Nobel ordered to be distributed annually as monetary awards in the areas of physics, literature, medicine, chemistry and peace.

For over a century the prestigious Nobel Prizes have been awarded with much acclaim each year. Annually the names of distinguished individuals from around the globe become heralded and immortalized for their achievements that advance progress in the world.

Today Nobel's lasting legacy stands solidly as a man who promoted and honored the very best in science, progress in the humanities, and the pursuit of peace.

It would appear that the true winner of the prize proved to be Alfred Nobel, now viewed eternally as a benefactor to peace and humanity.

Few will receive the opportunity to preview their obituary in the newspaper. Nevertheless, like Nobel, everyone possesses the ability to examine the fruits of their life and determine their legacy.

16
All the Way to the Top
May 2001 C.E.

On the morning of May 25, 2001, school teacher Erik Weihenmeyer of Golden, Colorado, stepped to the top of the world, and achieved a major milestone. The world's tallest peak, Mount Everest, looms forbiddingly at 29,035 feet dominating the Himalayas, the highest mountain range on earth. Augustly revered by the people of Nepal as Sagarmartha, "the goddess of the sky", this breathtaking, imperial pinnacle has inspired both awe and trepidation since time immemorial.

Surmounting the highest point on the planet stands a daunting achievement for anyone to attempt. To stand at the top means to straddle a narrow backbone of ice, snow and fragmented shale faced with a precipitous 10,000 foot vertical fall into Tibet on one flank and a treacherous 7,000 foot drop into Nepal on the other. Every moment on the mountain is perilous. At 29,000 feet, the Everest peak emerges into a continuous jet stream with brutally, cold, savage winds that can exceed 100 miles per hour. At high altitudes, oxygen deprivation causes the human body to go haywire, the heart to fluctuate wildly and internal organs begin to shut down. In the brain, mental processing becomes disoriented and severely altered. And even if every faculty were agile, any false step could hurtle a climber thousands of feet straight down sheer cliffs to their doom.

For a millennia reaching the top was deemed impossible until 1953 when Sir Edmund Hillary and Tenzing Norkay became the first to conquer the towering and immutable peak. In the 50 years following, Mount Everest remained obdurate, exacting the ultimate price from one in nine of those aspiring to attain her perilous heights. Though 59 bodies were reclaimed from the treacherous icy slopes, nearly 120 corpses reside for eternity; lost beneath the endless snows of the great peak.

When Erik Weihenmeyer made his attempt on Everest he ranked as no newcomer to mountain climbing. His previous conquests included Tanzania's Mount Kilimanjaro, 19,340 feet, Alaska's Mount McKinley at 20,320 feet, and Argentina's Mount Aconcagua, 22,834 feet. Following his astonishing feat on Everest, Erik soon completed his goal to successfully scale the highest peaks on all seven continents.

So what escalates Erik's ascents to the realm of incredible?

This simple fact: Erik is blind.

At age 13, he lost his sight completely to retinoscheses, a rare unraveling of the retinas. Undaunted, Erik began rock climbing at age 16. He accelerated his daring as the years progressed to include skydiving with his endeavors. At age 32, he sought and surmounted the greatest mountain known to the world and to mankind.

Aside from raw courage, determination and stamina, what enabled a man without sight to accomplish where so many others with the advantage of their eyes had failed?

The answer?   ...bells.

Erik's companions and the assisting Sherpa guides would carry one or more Alaskan bear bells attached to their backpack or ice pick. By listening to the ringing of the bells, Erik could ascertain direction and details in the guides' movements, and how he should set to follow with his ascent.

There are countless mountains, both real and imagined. Many appear to loom much greater than Everest...or blindness. And we immediately turn away, considering them insurmountable in our lives. Focusing on difficulties and drawbacks, we quickly succumb to hardship, accept inability or surrender to disability. Perhaps we look at the goal and simply believe it is too high.

Yet there are those who ascertain the circumstances and conditions, then resolutely move forward toward their peaks and goals. They innovate and improve. They not only surmount, but also greatly surpass these mountains that would halt others.

Mountains emerge in everyone's life. And in a real sense, we are all disabled in some way, be it a physical sense or a psychological one. How we face and surmount those barriers determine our character and the destination for our lives. Such bell by bell, step by step thinking got Erik Weihenmeyer literally to the top of the world.

Who would have thought to conquer the highest mountain on the planet...

...the ringing of little bells.

Don't concentrate on the mountain. There can be incredibly simple solutions to surmount mountainous complexities, and then reach those lofty pinnacles.

And soon the bells will be pealing; enabling the steps needed to make it all the way to the top.

17
Leading By Example
1776 C.E.

"Come on! Get your backs into it! Move that thing NOW!" the corporal yelled. Fuming, he stood and watched in frustration. His own command, a squad of four American soldiers were engaged mightily in trying to move a huge piece of timber blocking the trail. The way had to be cleared for severely needed Continental Army supply wagons to pass without delay.

Pacing impatiently, the corporal glanced across the snowy Pennsylvania countryside. Although it appeared pretty and pristine, its beauty and stillness escaped him entirely. All he viewed portended trouble and reminded him of previous difficulties. It had been bad weather all around in that year of 1778, he mused. And the colonies' continual setbacks and losses in the war with England had been as bad as the weather. Suddenly through the trees in the distance, he noted movement coming up the road. "Blast! Not the supply wagons already!" he growled to himself as he swung about and again verbally entreated his charges to hurry their labors.

As the men sweated and struggled, the corporal off to the side, continued to pace back and forth increasing his stride and ire. Could he ever hope for promotion in rank in this army if he couldn't even manage to get his small band to accomplish simple, but vital tasks like the clearing of a road? And now the whole supply line may be approaching. Important officers would view that he did not have command of the situation or the control of his men. In an effort to sound more authoritative, he drew himself up as one of the superior officers might look, and gave yet another loud and lordly order as the men toiled with the unyielding tree trunk, "PUSH!" It was to no avail. The corporal turned away for a moment and sighed dejectedly at his dilemma.

The chill evening breeze began to bite with a slight smattering of snow flurries drifting about. The corporal drew his cloak tighter about him and glanced at the steel gray skies. It promised more hard weather to come. Time is short, he reckoned. This assignment is impossible. How can I get these men motivated to move this tree in time?

Remembering the movement on the path, the corporal turned to identify it and track its progress. Only a lone rider on horseback rode up

the frosty, snow covered forest trail. The corporal hissed a searing breath
of relief at the sight. The horseman stopped before the squad of soldiers,
studying them as they continued working to push the heavy piece of
timber from the roadway. As the men grunted and struggled, the
corporal, too perturbed at the situation took little interest in the rider.
Covered in his winter cloak, the horseman quietly watched their labors for
several minutes. Finally he spoke to the officer.

"Why don't you help them?" he quietly asked, addressing the
corporal.

"Me?" the young officer replied incredulously. "Why, I'm a
corporal, sir!"

"Would you mind if I assist?" the horseman asked.

"If you can get this tree moved, then please do."

Dismounting, the stranger tethered his horse and approached the
soldiers. The four men took a moments' respite as the stranger surveyed
the situation and made suggestions to them about where they might place
themselves, work as a team and lift the tree. Pivot it first he indicated;
then it can be swiveled over and removed from the path. The stranger
looked to the young officer for his approval of the strategy. Since little
else was working, the annoyed corporal waved him on allowing the
stranger to try the approach.

The men placed themselves. The stranger's presence seemed to
motivate them and he himself strained with the tree. "Now, ALL
TOGETHER, BOYS...HEAVE!" he encouraged. With a groan the big
timber swiveled, slid, and tumbled off the road. The soldiers gave a shout
of joy with their success and turned to thank the stranger for his
assistance and instruction. Even the corporal had to stifle a well-placed
howl of happiness. In turn the stranger showed appreciation, taking time
to thank each soldier for their hard work and loyalty to the American
cause. The corporal stood back and smiled to himself. The road now
stood cleared in a timely manner. When the supply wagons rolled
through, his superiors would see his merit as an up-and-coming officer.
His frustration now dissipated, he beamed proudly at the thought and
even smiled at his squad for a moment. He then turned his attention to
the horseman.

The stranger had returned and mounted his horse. Beginning to
ride onward, he smiled and waved at the corporal. Then he halted
momentarily, pondering before he turned his steed and briefly addressed
the officer.

"Corporal, the next time you have a piece of timber for your men to handle, send for the commander-in-chief."

Suddenly, the dumbstruck young man realized his impatience had blinded him.

The horseman was George Washington.

One man gave orders. The other offered solutions and assistance. One man was a little more important than his peers and lost track of its meaning. The other man was supremely important and gladly worked along side his fellows. One man had a will. The other showed willingness. Two contrasting styles: one seeks to manage…seeing a task and people as parts in that task. The other leads by encouragement, example and empowerment. The people including himself, formed a team…and the task was accomplished.

George Washington happened to be a mediocre general, but a truly great leader. He lost most of his military engagements and battles. However his true measure of eminence came with his willingness to contribute at even the most basic level; to endure even the worst hardships alongside his troops. He demonstrated and inspired supreme devotion; the utmost standard of loyalty that made the difference between defeat and the eventual victory…leading to the birth of a nation.

In any area of participation…

What is your style? Management or Leadership?

18
Object of Limitless Possibilities
April 1940

The immense power of the invader's war machine had smothered their country with oppression. In spite of Norway declaring herself neutral at the beginning of World War II, other countries recognized that Norway's strategic location could not be ignored. The surprise attack by Germany on April 10, 1940 quickly overran the small, secluded nation. The state leadership, national treasury and Norway's King Haarkon VII, barely made an escape to England. Stunned by the lightening speed of the invasion, the citizens of Norway stood helpless as 375,000 German soldiers soon swarmed across the landscape, controlling the native population of 3 million.

The German military swiftly commandeered airports, air bases, and sea ports quickly converting them for use in future aggression against North Atlantic shipping and Allied naval movements. Dredging and expansion of shipping harbors adapted them for use by hostile battleships and submarine warfare, controlling the seas from the arctic to the coast of France. The defeated and dominated Norway would serve the Nazis superbly as a staging area for further planned invasions.

Throughout the cities and towns, the conquerors immediately imposed a brutal iron fist rule on Norway's population, strongly designed to inflict psychological subjugation. The new puppet leadership forced enrollment of all teachers, labor unions and remaining government officials into its Nazi social movement. All media was halted, churches closed and any public gatherings were suppressed. Fascism took root, placing all Norway under its boot.

In a final masterstroke, every symbol of Norway was removed. Flags, plaques, and medallions were stripped from all buildings, both public and private. Paper money and official stationary were destroyed. Even Norway's coins bearing government emblems were confiscated. Everything and anything representative of Norway vanished.

Although they dare not up-rise or speak against the Germans, the faithful and defiant citizens devised clever undercurrent methods of displaying nationality, solidarity, and protest. Numerous Norwegian coins still flourished in the possession of the citizenry. Suddenly the latest trend in fashion jewelry abounded with the king's image as wearing money rapidly gained attractiveness. The Nazi backlash descended immediately and brutally. All coin ornamentation was seized and those flaunting it ended up arrested.

The Norwegians refused to bow down. Soon a new style of chic charms emerged, a special jewelry created with the king's initials "KH7" for King Haarkon VII. They briefly thrived, adorning collars and lapels. The Nazis viciously hammered again, forbidding the display of jewelry or any outward promotion of the monarchy. No more warnings. Enforcing the ruling, the penalty was now arrest and death. Jewelry of any kind subsequently found its way into Nazi possession at this point. The people were left with nothing to fight back.

Not to be outdone, the Norwegians quietly revolted against their oppressors with the most readily available item they could find to show their defiance. Not even the Germans could confiscate all of these. These items subtly served as a source of Norwegian national pride and patriotism; an understated way of protesting against the tyranny of the Nazis. The new symbol of Norway seemed omnipresent. Even the thought of elimination proved impossible since the item presented itself everywhere. And every time the Germans saw or used this item, it offered simple defiance.

The citizens knew…and knew the Germans knew that this simple little 19th century invention had its origin in Norway. Worn as a source of pride and dissent against the Nazis, it infuriated the invaders so much that any person seen wearing it on their person was subject to immediate arrest. But the Norwegians continued wearing them. Turning up everywhere in the form of necklaces, bracelets, tie-tacks or brooches; some people even simply attached a small one to a hem or collar. The loyal Norwegians defiantly wore them to symbolize their solidarity and indomitable spirit. And the Nazis, a culture predicated on orderliness and mountains of official paperwork found themselves shackled to the same item. What could be done when a simple, unobtrusive, omnipresent item suddenly becomes a national symbol of unity? The Norwegian's answer to the Nazi's monumental attempt at iron gauntlet suppression and elimination the nation's spirit turned tables on the invaders.

World War II ended in 1945 and Norway regained its freedom. What had become a psychological weapon and the country's national symbol in the most desperate of times they cast as a giant 23 foot tall statue which now stands in Oslo, Norway's capital.

Over 60 years later, scholars still assert the little tool remains the most useful invention in history.

In his book: *"Elegant Solutions: Quintessential Technology for a User-Friendly World"*, Owen Edwards states, "If all that survives our fatally flawed civilization is (this same item used by Norway), archaeologists from some galaxy far, far away may give us more credit than we deserve. In our vast catalog of material innovation, no more perfectly conceived object exists."

High praise indeed.

The basic appearance of the tool suggests sleekness and the transformation into more imaginative forms and functions. Created and patented almost simultaneously in Norway and the United States in 1898-99, this remarkable invention stands so perfected that it has remained fundamentally unchanged for a over a century. No attempt at improving it has taken hold. New designs, materials and colors come and go but the essential item remains both intact and widely in use.

This product sparks creativity and practical inventive application. Research reveals only one in ten of these remarkable gadgets ever finds use in its designed purpose. Ubiquitous, this invention rapidly became and continues to be among the most basic staples of business...any kind of business anywhere around the globe.

With the myriad of in-a-pinch uses and possibilities, this invention may at this very moment hold together a variety of the mechanical machinery in the world. People have utilized them as both toothpick and lock pick. Some of them fashion as a cleaner for everything from sink drains to human ears. They have been effectively wielded as weapons. Their tactile nature in terms of size, shape and material has made them a prime source of use for the release of stress, tension, frustration, anticipation and aggression. Women have found them useful for assorted purposes including fasteners for bras, holders of straps, securing elements for pants, even closures for blouses. Men have enlisted them as tie clasps and gambling chips in card games. They are popular markers in children's games too.

And perhaps that is the point. This invention proves the astonishing diversity of human inventiveness; the limitless functions a single, simple vehicle can provide.

Where can one of these amazing creations be found? Perhaps one sits right now within arm's reach. Yes, that elementary, elongated, circular strip of wire…the humble paper clip.

Imagine, if something so simple can so exceed mere function in so many situations, consider the potential in something so far greater…
…like yourself.

19
Hail the Conquering Hero
February, 1928 C.E.

Through 13 tense years of saber rattling, pressuring, and jockeying for position, Haile Selassie managed a precarious rise to the throne of Ethiopia. As prince regent under his cousin, the Empress Zauditu, he built considerable influence and acted as ruler "de facto".

The Empress realized she held no real power and finally abdicated the throne, proclaiming Selassie as Emperor in 1928. His progressive outlook, particularly toward international trade, unsettled high-level leaders in the tradition laden country. Many powerful regional governors, each with their own army, preferred Selassie's predecessor, the Empress, who had held with the old ways and philosophy. To solidify his new position and unite the nation, Selassie immediately commanded each provincial governor in the country to journey to the capital and pledge allegiance to him.

All eventually responded except one. This prominent, outspoken, final opponent, Dejazmatch Balcha Saffo, powerful Governor of the wealthy province of Sidamo, refused the command to journey to the Ethiopian capital, Addis Ababa. When former Empress Zauditu requested Balcha's presence, Balcha realized the occasion provided the perfect opportunity to display his own power and authority. Perhaps his pressure might force Selassie to return the throne to Empress Zauditu.

In February of 1928, the fierce territorial leader Balcha assembled an army of 10,000 hardened mercenaries and boldly made way to the city. A seasoned and prestigious military commander, Balcha had prepared should he be stepping into a trap. Well protected, he could choose to ignite a civil war with this armed multitude. Selassie dare not cross him. Setting up camp in the valley of Nifas Silk, three miles from the capital, Balcha sat back, assuming a vanquisher's role and attitude. It was an open and direct challenge to the new emperor. The governor patiently waited. Selassie could make the next move.

To the warlord's surprise, Selassie sent emissaries to the encampment the next day. After humbling themselves before Balcha and praising his strength and courage, Selassie's envoys respectfully asked the great warrior to attend an afternoon banquet to be held in Balcha's honor. It would be presented in the capital city and hosted by Selassie. Although it flattered him immensely, Balcha considered the offer suspiciously. He recognized this could be a trap. Once there and eventually drunk, his enemy could kill him.

However Balcha would outsmart his enemy's ruse. He accepted the invitation, planning to return to his troops in the valley by nightfall. Balcha demanded that his personal 600 man bodyguard accompany him to the banquet. To his satisfaction, his stipulation was met with the utmost politeness and the terms gladly accepted.

Balcha prepared. He ordered his bodyguards not to get drunk. They must keep their wits about them. Look for a trap. Be ready at a moment's notice. Yet when they arrived in force, Selassie proved disarmingly charming. It appeared obvious that the monarch desperately needed Balcha's support, approval and cooperation. The wily governor refused to be captivated, repeatedly threatening his host by defiantly boasting of his huge force prepared to attack the city if he did not return by nightfall. Selassie seemed taken aback with hurt feelings at the inference that he might harm his guest.

The banquet progressed lavishly. The celebration centered entirely upon Balcha. The entertainment focused completely upon Balcha. The songs of honor were all sung exclusively for Balcha. Even with the charm and compliments bestowed upon him, Balcha and his men retorted with defiance and insults. Yet no retaliation arose for their harshness. Eventually Balcha began to believe that Selassie truly feared him; that this diminutive man was genuinely intimidated by him and his reputation. If this new monarch desperately courting him stood as the last obstacle to Balcha's preferred sovereign, the Empress, there existed no need to worry. The mighty Balcha smugly entertained thoughts that with his help the Empress would soon control Ethiopia and tradition would be restored.

The event ended without incident. Balcha and his 600 men left the city confident of their obvious superiority; laughing and jeering about the slight little man who plied so hard to please them. They even began to devise their strategy to take the city and remove the monarch from power. So confident were they, plans began to be discussed regarding how they would victoriously parade through the streets afterward.

When Balcha crested the final hill to descend to his valley encampment however, something proved terribly amiss…

The entire army was gone.

Only the smoldering remnants of doused camp fires remained from his enormous, armed encampment. A single wandering witness happened by to tell the tale...

During the banquet, Selassie's army had encircled the 10,000 mercenaries. They then peaceably approached and generously offered to buy all aggressors' weapons for a top price in gold, treasure and coins. Knowing that Balcha would have heard any distant fighting if it occurred, Selassie's troops didn't fire a shot, nor did they allow the enemy to do so. Selassie's men simply bought every last weapon. Even those few initially refusing to sell were eventually convinced.

Balcha's main force consisted of hardened mercenaries; therefore Selassie knew that greed would overcome what small loyalty actually existed. A quick profit without risk weighed infinitely superior to violent confrontation with questionable success or survival. Within a very short time, Balcha's entire force had been calmly disarmed and scattered to the winds, pleased and content with their money. Balcha had been fully prepared to fight everything except the one element he could not predict: a base human nature and the innate greed of his mercenary soldiers who held no allegiance.

Having disposed of Balcha's massive armed horde, Selassie's army now guarded the only exits from the narrow valley, entrapping Balcha and his remaining 600 men. Even then with Balcha at his mercy, Selassie proved to be a man of honor. Instead of executing his foe, the new emperor generously allowed Balcha to disburse his remaining men. The governor himself was allowed to retire to a very distant and extremely remote monastery...for the remainder of his life.

Strong and thought out resolutions to problems, backed with strength and resolve can win the day without use of force.

20
Won't Get Fooled Again
1799 C.E.

Normally efficient and focused, the eminent British scientific authorities had a hearty guffaw at the specimen recently submitted for authentication as a new species.

The late 18th century had been a tremendous time of exploration and discovery for the expanding global British Empire. The year, 1799, appeared no exception. A British survey team had returned from the mysterious, far flung island of Tasmania with exceptional and highly exotic samples of minerals, fish, fowl, mammal and reptiles. The amazing flora and fauna, alien to anything previously seen, were submitted to the British Museum along with exacting observation journals, detailed sketchbooks, and meticulous, analytical diaries for study. Captain John Hunter, the leader of this latest voyage, had presented the strange little creature that may have caused the scientists to check the calendar to see if April Fool's Day had changed this year.

The well respected and dignified British authorities had previously been bamboozled by clever shams. Chinese merchants found profit in "assisting" western explorers in uncovering new discoveries. As greater discoveries meant greater wealth to be gained, detection evolved into creation. Well known for their skill at stitching together faux hybrid creatures, the clever Chinese marketers gained a reputation for foisting elaborate frauds. Subsequently, the museum had sustained red faced embarrassment, widespread mockery in the press, and public ridicule over quick authentication of fakes. Having already been ensnared by various deceptions, these learned British pillars of science had vowed they would not be fooled again.

Before naturalist George Shaw, Keeper of the Department of Natural History at the British Museum and his associates lay a deceased, small furry animal about 2 feet in length. The voyage observation book noted an official Latin classification name: Ornithorhynchus anatinus. As they dissected the alleged specimen, the doctors marveled at the seamless assembly and superior craftsmanship of the counterfeit. Apparently parts of a half dozen different species had been carefully crafted to resemble a singular beast.

It had thick, grey-brown fur and a wide, flat tail like a beaver. While it sported four feet, they were fully webbed as if the feet of a waterfowl. The furry head ended in a wide, flat beak like a Mallard. Dissection of the brain revealed it to be single hemisphere, common to reptiles. Akin to snake fangs, the creature carried two large, venomous spurs behind the rear ankles which secreted poison. Noting the many, minute details, the scientists admired the outstanding, anonymous effort to trump them.

Compounding the scientists' doubt, the supposed diaries lent highly suspect details of the questionable animal's lifestyle and habits. They made more fanciful reading than a child's fairy tale.

Allegedly, this critter:

- Growled like a dog.
- Lived in bodies of water, but had been seen to climb trees.
- Gave birth by laying eggs similar to a bird or reptile, but always two at a time, no more and no less.
- Acted akin to a mammal and fed the hatched babies with milk. Yet there were no nipples. Supposedly, the milk emanated from tiny slits and the youngsters licked it off the mother's fur.
- Stuck to a diet consisting of select worms dredged from the bottoms of ponds.
- Acted much like a squirrel that stores nuts in its cheeks. Since the singular diet of worms could prove scarce, this wondrous little creature used pouches in its cheeks to store live worms for future needs.

Despite the apparent sham, Shaw dutifully examined the creature and published a detailed description of the specimen in the scientific journal *Naturalist's Miscellany*. He confessed, "…impossible not to entertain some doubts as to the genuine nature of the animal, and to surmise that there might have been practised some arts of deception in its structure."

Other experts involved in the post mortem study chimed in equally condescending that the creature provided an elaborate fake. British surgeon Robert Knox, a member of the museum, explained in his report that because the specimens arrived in England via the Indian Ocean, naturalists suspected Chinese sailors as the culprits. "Aware of the monstrous impostures which the artful Chinese had so frequently practiced on European adventurers," Knox noted, "the scientific authorities felt inclined to class this rare production of nature with eastern mermaids and other works of art."

Thus, after thoroughly examining the evidence, the British Museum scientists publicly announced they had come to an absolute and unanimous conclusion: This was a hoax of the first order. The British Museum staff congratulated themselves to have nipped the silliness in the bud; smugly agreed that their comprehensive analysis proved their scholarly superiority while avoiding being made fools of once again.

However in 1804, a group of explorers in the Australian territory of New South Wales came upon a large pond positively teeming with the bizarre creatures. The crew returned to England with several live specimens; dubbing them the "duck-billed platypus".

Focused on the consequences of previous experience, the eminent scientists had succumbed to a closed mind. They took what they *knew* and refused something *new*.

Even in absolute certainty allow room for the unexpected.

21
Fighting Words
1917 C.E.

The British were persistent about it. The Americans did not believe it. The Mexicans refused it. The Germans created it, sent it and unfortunately, defended it.

In the end, it, a few instructions on a brief telegraph message sent in early 1917, ignited the ire of the pacifist, isolationist-minded American public and swayed the final results of World War I, 1914-1918; the Great War.

By the height of World War I in 1916, combat still roiled across Europe between the Allied and Central Powers. Precious lives and valuable manpower continued to be offered up for wholesale destruction through endless, futile, indecisive battles. Casualties mounted into the millions with the Allies suffering triple the human loss. Measurable success between the combatants had all but ground to a stalemate, a few yards of land continually forfeited back and forth. Both sides looked beyond their borders for any means to tip the scales toward a win in their favor. Yet far across the Atlantic Ocean the American government and citizens remained adamant for peace and secure in their isolationism.

Half a world away from the world's worst conflagration American President Woodrow Wilson pledged that this massive war of destruction would not involve his hemisphere. In November, 1916, Wilson won re-election on the slogan, "He kept us out of the Great War."

President Wilson promoted negotiations for peaceable cessation of hostilities between the warring parties in Europe: the Allied (Entente) powers—England, France, Russia, Australia, Canada, Italy, and the Central powers—Germany, Austria-Hungary, the Ottoman Empire, and Bulgaria. In offering a neutral hand, he opened the U.S. government's diplomatic telegraph lines between Sweden and Washington D.C. for confidential use to both Allied and Central powers. In his inaugural address on March 5, 1917, Wilson proclaimed, "We desire neither conquest nor advantage. We wish nothing that can be had only at the cost of another people. We always professed unselfish purpose and we covet the opportunity to prove our professions are sincere." Pacifism ruled in United States of America.

President Wilson continued to promote negotiations for peaceable cessation of hostilities between the warring parties in Europe: the Allied (Entente) powers—England, France, Russia, Australia, Canada, Italy, and the Central powers—Germany, Austria-Hungary, the Ottoman Empire, and Bulgaria. In offering a neutral hand, he opened the U.S. government's diplomatic telegraph lines between Sweden and Washington D.C. for confidential use to both Allied and Central powers. In his inaugural address on March 5, 1917, Wilson proclaimed, "We desire neither conquest nor advantage. We wish nothing that can be had only at the cost of another people. We always professed unselfish purpose and we covet the opportunity to prove our professions are sincere."

Backing his election promise, Wilson systematically began staffing reductions amongst the already sketchy U.S. Military of 138,000 soldiers. Numerically the United States Army already ranked smaller than the Lithuanian militia of that same era. Not only limited in manpower, the U.S. military proved sadly deficient in every aspect of then-modern warfare. The army lacked even an intelligence and code-breaking unit. Its existing staff and leadership were neither prepared nor cognizant to cope with the logistical and operational problems to be presented by major conflict.

In an evaluation of the aid U.S. soldiers might add if enticed to the Allied cause, the chief of the British Imperial General Staff commented in February, 1917, "I do not think that it will make much difference whether America comes in or not. What we want to do is to beat the German Armies, until we do that we shall not win the war. America will not help us much in that respect." Documentation indicates the French concurred. All parties, even the Germans and Americans, conceded it would take the U.S. an entire year to assemble, train and deploy a poorly equipped, sparse army of just 250,000 soldiers. Small potatoes when the British had lost 60,000 combat-hardened soldiers in the first day of the five month long Battle of the Somme. A million soldiers would perish in that one battle alone.

Private companies in the United States like Colt, Ford, Remington, Winchester and others used U.S. neutrality to their advantage, supplying both sides of the conflict with food, uniforms, boots, equipment and guns. In slightly over two years of war the U.S. had received $850 million from Britain in return for munitions and provisions plus an additional $169 million from Germany. Staying neutral proved to be "good business".

However by 1916, the Central powers viewed the economic involvement of the United States as bad business. Across Europe, Imperial Germany could see the glimmer of final victory on the horizon. The unity of the Allied powers in Europe had shifted, unraveling in disarray. The French troops initiated widespread mutiny after suffering 75% casualties. Forced by pre-existing treaties to enter the war, the Italian government and military now faltered from their losses. Russian Czar Nicolas II, abdicated as his nation faced the upheavals of Communist revolution. Of the European Allies, Britain appeared to now stand nearly alone. With their current stockpiles, the German armies could well outlast the British. And on the chance that U.S. exports to England were to cease, the scales would tip in the German Empire's favor. Victory, success and power nearly danced within Germany's grasp.

A quiet but bold tactic unfolded to insure the Americans would become fully self-occupied on their own continent; a plan set to cause the U.S. to withdraw war-related exports and to keep her away from hostilities in Europe. On January 16, 1917, Arthur Zimmermann, the German Foreign Secretary, dispatched a highly confidential directive to the German legation in Mexico.

The telegram instructed Germany's head of legation in Mexico to form a clandestine agreement of alliance between Germany and Mexico. Should the United States fail to maintain neutrality due to Germany's blatant submarine attacks against neutral ships, the plan called for Mexico to attack the United States along the U.S. borders of New Mexico, Texas and Arizona, a distance of 1,000 miles. This ploy would fully engage the limited U.S. military and bring redirection of U.S. exported manufactured supplies to the border conflict. In return, Mexico could reconquer and occupy Arizona, New Mexico and Texas; territory forfeited in the Mexican/American war of 1848. To support and insure Mexico's effort and success, Germany would quietly supply Mexico the finances for the advanced infantry weaponry to pursue the attack and invasion.

Confident of the waning U.S. military status, Germany envisioned Mexico trumping the U.S. Border States in an assault. Germany would benefit with an enlarged and empowered Mexico as their strong ally. With dwindling supplies, the British army would fail, and Germany, herself busy with a war on the other side of the world would not be suspect. And should the United States suddenly see a reason to join the war, there would be no war to fight in the time it would take them to mobilize an army of any consequence. Proud of her excellent strategy, Germany felt almost giddy. Impervious and simple; the plan merely needed to remain covert and confidential.

Severed undersea cables, courtesy of the British navy at the start of the war, prohibited Germany from telegraphing Mexico directly. Instead, Zimmermann audaciously transmitted his confidential missive through the U.S. diplomatic lines sequestered exclusively for peace negotiations. Secure in his country's latest encryption code, German foreign secretary Zimmermann sent his encoded telegram boldly to the German emissary in Washington D.C. with instructions to pass it on to Mexico. The Germans were fearless.

The German ambassador to the U.S. flashed his credentials, and was handed the telegraphed page listing numerous sets of ordered numbers. Hustling back to the embassy, he sequestered himself, laboring personally to translate the provocative telegram. Before forwarding the incendiary cable to the Mexico head of the legation as instructed, he carefully re-encrypted it in a different cipher.

On the flip side, Britain also knew that covert and confidential reigned supreme. They had already captured and decoded the cable on its way to Washington D.C. The English government now knew of the plot, and the brilliant opportunity before them to rally the United States into their war with Germany.

The British desperately wanted to reveal the incriminating telegram exposing the German plan to bring the U.S. homeland under attack, but faced a great dilemma. If Britain boldly produced the actual telegram, the Americans would recognize the British had the snagged the correspondence as it passed through the diplomatic telegraph lines.

How could they unleash the damning note without revealing they were spying on the very nation they hoped would commit to their cause? Yet if the provocative missive did not become public knowledge, England would lose a promising prospect to draw the United States into the war on the side of the Allies.

How could the British reveal the note to incite and inflame the American righteous indignation?

Mulling over the problem, English military intelligence realized that due to the severed cables, Germany had been forced to use Washington D.C. as a carom to reach Mexico. Since no other cable options lay available to Germany, the ambassador would forward the message to Mexico via Western Union. ...That was it!!! A copy of the telegram could exist along the route to Mexico City's public telegraph office! Shouts reverberated through the halls of British naval intelligence as Admiral "Blinker" Hall, director, leapt to action, launching his foreign agents in pursuit of the cable by hook or crook, bribery or theft.

On February 23, 1917, the British foreign secretary proudly presented the decoded contents of the incriminating telegram to the U.S. Ambassador to Britain. Quickly, he relayed it to U.S. President Woodrow Wilson.

British confidence zoomed. The timing of the forwarded message couldn't be more perfect. Nearly 200 American lives had recently perished in the unrelenting German submarine attacks on neutral vessels.

But suddenly the British plan soured. The American government would not budge from its path for "Peace without Victory". Undeterred, allies of the English sought the next best route...newspapers. On March 1, 1917, a copy of the telegram went to the world press. Yet that too backfired. Shocked and disbelieving, the American public rejected the telegram as a fraud designed to lure them into the war on the British side. German and Mexican diplomats immediately launched campaigns vociferously proclaiming their innocence; both strongly supported by pro-German U.S. organizations, the ACLU, and other American peace movements. All denounced the telegram as a forgery, and the English as vile tricksters.

Stumped, the British felt they had reached an impasse when they were shocked to learn of a strange turnabout arising from the most unlikely source. In an unexpected move, German Foreign Secretary Arthur Zimmermann, the author of the very telegram in question, confirmed its authenticity in two, separate public speeches.

Perhaps in a strategic effort to allay any potential distrust from the U.S. toward Germany, Zimmerman defended that his telegram had not called for attacks on the United States. "..I declared expressly that, despite the submarine war, we hoped that America would maintain neutrality. My instructions were to be carried out only after the United States had declared war...I believe the instructions were absolutely loyal as regards to the United States...and as the great mass of American people, saw there was nothing to object to in these instructions... newspapers felt obliged to admit regretfully that not so very much had been made out of this affair."

Zimmermann also faulted President Wilson for having earlier broken diplomatic relations with Germany "with extraordinary roughness", leaving Zimmermann to plead Germany's victimization alone because they "no longer had the opportunity to explain the German attitude, and that the U.S. government had declined to negotiate." He solemnly concluded, "Thus I considered it a patriotic duty to release those instructions…"

The British were stunned by the turn of events and the source of their good fortune.

Zimmermann's speeches occurred March 23rd and 29th, 1917.

The United States entered the war mere days later on April 6th.

A motivated America raised, trained and deployed a well-equipped army of 4 million soldiers to Europe in less than 17 months, by June, 1918.

The war ended with the surrender of Germany four months later, November 11th, 1918.

Like a slumbering Grizzly awakened from hibernation and roaring its presence, the United States emerged from the early 20th Century World War I as a military superpower, and remains a global strength today, channeling world affairs in the 21st century.

So, what in the world went wrong?

Germany, confident the United States stood firmly pacifist, isolationist, and wholly ineffective militarily, moved forward with a plan that was logical, factual, and achievable; seemingly foolproof. Yet that practical view was quickly steamrolled by a passion that Germany could never have anticipated.

The one factor they had not realized reveals itself in a popular U.S. war song written days after war was declared:

Over there. Over there.
Send the word, send the word over there.
That the Yanks are coming, the Yanks are coming.
The drums rum-tumming ev'rywhere.
So prepare, say a pray'r,
Send the word, send the word to beware.
We'll be over, we're coming over,
And we won't come back till it's over,
Over There.

The comprehension that Germany intended to bring the brutal European conflagration onto their U.S soil aroused a fierce fury in the U.S. populace. Germany had no inkling the message of the telegram would ignite such passion; that America would wield all of its power and be willing to sacrifice everything to keep the conflict "Over There."

Within months, the tables turned on Germany. In losing the war, Germany lost her military, her traditional government, her territory, her economy, and her heart.

"The end justifies the means." In today's society, the slogan provides acceptable excuse for underhanded manipulation towards a self-gratifying end. Be very aware, as learned by Germany in a hard way, those means can completely change the envisioned end.

22
Obvious Intent
1904 C.E.

It was simply titled, the "Infant Incubator."

A thinly masked freak show, this early 1900's exhibit consisted of a large room lined with rows of infant incubators arrayed in full public display. Each glass cubicle contained a breathtakingly diminutive baby, fighting to live. Women dressed as nurses directed and moved throngs of entranced, paying patrons along the viewing walkways while enthralling them with morbid tidbits about each struggling, premature nursling. People lined up in droves, paying to peruse the tiny "preemies" wriggle and writhe on the desperate border between life and death.

In the summer of 1904 in the very heart of New York's legendary entertainment extravaganza known simply as Coney Island, the grandest amusement park ever conceived, Dreamland first opened its glorious gates. The lavish, $3.5 million stellar attraction with its ornate towers and enticing midway offered anything one could possibly imagine for entertainment. Amidst the hoopla and hype, millions of lights, roaring roller coasters, carnival barkers and the strange, fascinating collection of often revolting freak shows, the most popular, repeatedly patronized pavilion proved to be the Infant Incubator.

Scorned as a "baby hatchery" by condescending local hospitals, the show ignited strong protests by child-cruelty organizations for being "grossly unsafe" and "immorally placing infants in public display". Turn of the century detractors derided the vulgar charade as the very far edge of bad taste. One 1901, newspaper article described the distasteful pageant as "Tiny creatures living in artificial glass houses in full view for all to visually gape and ogle".

In spite of the apparent affront and contempt toward common decency, the amusement park sideshow persisted, creating avid devotees, many of them childless women. Continuing to arrive daily by the thousands, fans paid the then-exorbitant price of a dime to stand and view the wrinkled, runty human infants hover helplessly near doom. Many made weekly treks to scrutinize the imminent death or analyze the possible survival by their next visit on any number of the palm-sized beings struggling before them. The mawkish and disconcerting sight of the preemies, daily thrust brazenly into the limelight for all to gawk and prattle over also incurred official disdain and condemnation for the depraved founder.

Repeatedly branded as a sham doctor, the man who created this offensive sideshow display of helpless humanity for profit had already evaded several lawsuits. Demands of money from event proprietors at major fairgrounds for his earlier, similar spectacles still haunted his steps. What kind greedy showman could sink so low? How heartless can such a monster be?

...Who was he?

Dr. Martin Couney, an American Medical Association member and respected researcher, originated the display of premature babies in incubators. In spite of its location, the exhibit sought to maintain a quiet, working hospital setting for the viewing of pre-mature birth infants. Yes, watching dwarfish newborns drift vulnerably near mortality may seem ghoulish but it brought to the public's attention the plight of thousands of children who were often abandoned to die at birth.

Dr. Couney's venture proved to skeptics and hospitals the value of the stigmatized incubator in saving infant lives. He breached social frontiers by providing care without regard to a child's race, social or economic status. He was unconcerned with the ethnic or religious background of the parents, or even any knowledge of the parents—an offense and shock to most people one hundred years ago. The dimes of his unique patrons paid for the annual operating costs, staff, plus obtained medical attention for the survival of these forsaken infants without use of charity, begging, or pleading.

The bottom line? The Infant Incubator became the most consistently popular exhibit at two amusement centers, Luna Park and Dreamland. It outlasted both parks, surviving nearly 40 years at Coney Island to the point where the location occasioned reference as "Couney Island". It endured despite the scorn, derision, condemnation and legal attempts to obliterate it. Through the years, the proceeds of this macabre exhibit saved 7,500 of the 8,500 children placed on display. The little freak-show, open only during the traditional summer amusement season saved the lives of thousands of New York City children during its existence.

A Freak Show and a Monster...

There are times the obvious is not obvious. The facade will not always show the true heart of the matter. However the wise will see… and recognize the difference.

23
Height of Fame
September18, 1932 C.E.

The stars beckoned brightly that clear September evening. From the shadows she emerged, an absolute vision of loveliness in the luminous moonlight; elegantly dressed in a stunning, flowing gown and treading her measured steps in fashionable high heels. With her brilliant blonde hair coifed to perfection and impeccable makeup enhancing her beautiful face, she presented the exquisite image to which every movie starlet aspires.

She appeared to float along, gliding silently as puffs of gentle night breezes softly swirled her gossamer attire. Having had a long and deliberated debate with herself, Peg Entwistle had made her choice. She would leave her mark on Hollywood...

Born in 1908, Peg's father brought her to America from Wales when she was 14; her mother having died earlier. A stage performer himself, he set into motion Peg's fire, passion and quest for fame. In 1925, at the tender age of 17 she became one of the youngest actresses to star in a major Broadway production, a staging of *Hamlet*. By 1927, at the impressionable age of 19, she was involved in a string of Broadway hits with the prestigious New York City Theater Guild.

However fame often becomes fleeting and Peg's 1931-1932 season emerged a nightmare with eight failed productions in a row. She fell into deep depression, but still sought her shining star. By April of 1932 the glitter and glamour of Hollywood beckoned and Peg responded. With determination, she now looked west. She quickly garnered a stage role with the legendary Billie Burke now fondly remembered as Glinda, the Good Witch of the North in *The Wizard of OZ*. The two of them starred in a theatrical production called *The Mad Hopes*. That play also ended quickly.

A movie role followed in the mystery, *Thirteen Women*, starring Irene Dunne. Yet there too the early reviews turned sour and the movie went through extensive editing for re-release. Most of Peg's performance ended up on the cutting room floor. RKO studios did not renew her contract. Peg was devastated.

With no income, she relinquished her apartment and moved in with an uncle who resided on Beachwood Drive, right under the shadow of the world famous Hollywood sign. Things certainly looked bleak. Peg had been in the limelight and craved it deeply. Once there, like so many touched by stardom, there burned a yearning; a fierce need to be famous, to be noticed. After long thought and consideration, Peg Entwistle made her choice and determined she would leave her mark on Hollywood. By making a bold move this town would remember her.

Thus on the night of September 18, 1932, with the attention to her appearance of a Best Actress nominee about to attend the Academy Awards, the 24 year old Peg Entwistle donned her finest clothes. Every detail was perfect: her gloves, purse, jewelry, makeup, hair, stockings and heels. Peg looked her very best. She then embarked on a long, quiet stroll to the top of Beachwood Drive. Past the end of the street, she circumvented the retaining fence. Laboriously she struggled her way through brush and brambles up the steep and rugged hillside terrain. Reaching her goal, she paused to remove and neatly fold her coat, placing it on the ground along with her purse. Then in her gown and heels she arduously and slowly ascended, stepping up the many rungs of the maintenance ladder behind the 45 foot high letter H in the Hollywood sign. Straining, Peg climbed resolutely upward. She toiled purposefully nearly five stories until she reached the top…and stood, unwavering.

It is unknown how long the beautiful starlet remained there, bathed in the intense blaze of the sign's 4,000 brilliant spotlights illuminating her as she gazed over the city. While the noise and bright lights of Tinsel town flashed below her, the silent, alluring lights of the stars twinkled above calmly beckoning. Peg Entwistle chose to be a star. She dove into the darkness.

Her final effort achieved a measure of fame. She headlined the newspapers for days. Her purse proved empty save for a single page suicide note with only two lines handwritten upon it, ending with her initials…no name. Thus she lay unknown in the morgue for several days while newspapers pleaded with the public to identify the "Hollywood Sign Girl."

The final twist arrived the morning following her suicide. A letter addressed to her had been forwarded and delivered to her uncle's residence. Peg Entwistle had been offered the lead role in a new production at the Beverly Hills Playhouse.

Sadly, Peg Entwistle achieved her lasting fame. To this day she remains the only person to have committed suicide by leaping from the Hollywood sign.

Peg Entwistle had made her choice, and her mark on Hollywood. One wonders how they might have differed, had she delayed a single day.

Sometimes we feel unable to see beyond the night; forgetting that we cannot predict what the new dawn will bring. However no matter the circumstances, there exist choices. Life is full of choices, and life itself is a choice.

Peg's choice calls to mind another starlet's final line in Hollywood's famous film, *Gone With The Wind*. Scarlett O'Hara, having lost what she most desired exclaims:

"After all, tomorrow is another day."

24
Sign of the Times
2000 C.E.

In Oregon there lives a diminutive tan and white bird that instigated a firestorm of controversy between environmental groups and the lumber industry. For generations a major source of lumber in the United States has been the Pacific Northwest. Scores of jobs in that area, and actually the very economy itself, have been dependent upon the logging industry. Yet this small species known as the Northern Spotted Owl stood to bring it all to its knees.

Passionate preservation groups had reached defiant loggerheads with local logging interests in defense of the world's small number of remaining, known Northern Spotted Owls. The species according to environmental studies, would only nest in old growth timber 75 or more years in age. These rare birds resided in the same Pacific Northwest forests the logging interests sought to reap.

The clash raged on for years. In pursuit of some compromise, the logging groups offered to replant the owls' sanctuary with more trees than would be removed. This was not acceptable to the preservationists. They reasserted that the owls shunned the existing new-growth trees, reconfirming the view that the birds limited their nests to particular old-growth trees in the region. The opposition countered that the old-growth trees presented an inherent fire danger and possible threat to the owls. Nevertheless the environmentalists remained firm against any environmental changes: The species must be protected from extinction. Period.

After the battle had escalated to a national level drawing both media and government attention, there dawned one notable spring day in April 2000 in Medford, Oregon. Quite a crowd from both sides of the on-going issue had gathered in a large, urban parking lot. They stood, staring at each other and at what confronted them. Some were dumbfounded, others astounded, and many truly relieved. A resolution appeared to be at hand. Before them sat a member of this controversy; one of the rare Spotted Owls. The petite bird had comfortably nestled and nested…in the crux of the giant, red K of a discount mart's lighted sign.

In all their masses of scientific data, the one thing the die-hard environmentalists had apparently overlooked was the possibility of the species to change. The owl proved to be far more resilient, and in scientific circles became far more respected for its adaptability. As for choosing the location with the K...well perhaps there's just no accounting for taste.

Increasingly our world undergoes immense and rapid changes. Many times throughout past history, people, communities, cities and even entire civilizations were overcome or failed to survive due to physical, social, political, and environmental shocks that required tremendous transformation.

Like the Northern Spotted Owl and many other conditions in the natural world, political world, business world, and social world, the stories of the ones who do survive are noteworthy. However the stories of the ones who don't simply survive, but actually adapt and thrive in such dynamic situations become the tales that stand the test of time as lessons to us all. They capture the imagination of the world.

Although tradition and "old growth" can be comfortable, seek to incorporate new ways to accomplish old tasks. Be ready to forge ahead into change.

...And astonish those who would seek to brand you otherwise.

25
Leftover Rewards
1683 C.E.

It was an event that sought to change the entire history of Europe, but it failed…and it succeeded.

A massive army of 140,000 Islamic Turks under the command of Grand Vizier Kara Mustafa, launched from Istanbul in 1683. Separating himself from the Ottoman Turks, and to establish his own Islamic kingdom in order to declare himself as sultan, Mustafa had begun a march that swept unstoppable across Europe. Their swath of conquest suffered no defeats or even detours. Kara Mustafa's invasion had consumed the land from Istanbul, across Eastern Europe and now into Austria.

Finally the army came upon the last great bastion that stood in their way, the walled city of Vienna. If the Turks could take this fortress, the few remaining towns and villages on the continent would not likely slow them in their quest to conquer all of Europe.

With an immense supply caravan to sustain them, the Turks patiently set up a huge encampment around Vienna and began their siege of the city on July 17th, 1683, content to seal off the capital and wait for the opportune moment to attack.

By late August, Vienna's resistance was weakening and become futile as supplies dwindled. Unable to communicate with the rest of Europe, their hopes waned. On September 1st, their plight shifted to desperation as a well-placed explosive by the Turks destroyed a key portion of the outer wall. The invaders poured in and Vienna's defenders retreated behind secondary fortifications.

Someone had to go for help. But who dared brave infiltrating and passing through the vast, well-entrenched hostile forces? A young Polish mercenary named Jerzy Kulcyzcki stepped forward, volunteering to take the risk.

At dusk he began, quietly slipping outside the fortress. Artfully enacting the disguise of a Turkish soldier, the Pole cunningly blended into the massive enemy encampment. Adopting an air of nonchalance, he began his trek through the huge tent city that sprawled before him. Along the way he paused here and there, stopping to chat amicably at various campfires with the soldiers. Occasionally he even took the time to casually sit, eat and drink with them to dispel suspicion. At one cluster of soldiers, Kulcyzcki made a slip of the tongue. His identity was challenged! Arab tempers flared and wickedly-curved Turkish Scimitar blades immediately surrounded him, glinting in the firelight. Thinking quickly, Kulcyzcki smiled at his adversaries, continued sipping from his own cup and calmly offered to pour them another drink. He invited them to sit and resume their casual conversation as he confidently explained away the misunderstanding. Leaving on friendly terms, he moved on effortlessly. Continuing through the night he subtly, cautiously and steadily worked his way toward the outer edges, tent by tent, campfire by campfire.

Just before dawn he plied his progress to the edge of the encampment and slipped unseen into the dark forest beyond. Then as swiftly as his legs would carry him, he raced off to gain the help of his sovereign, King Jan Sobieski of Poland. Kulcyzcki knew the king maintained a large military, plus carried alliances with the Bavarian army for attacks such as this.

The morning of September 12th began with numerous explosions rocking and destroying the inner city walls. The city faced certain annihilation as the attackers began their final assault. The Turks started pouring through the gaps in the ruined walls. But then, literally in the nick of time, a rescuing army of 80,000 Bavarian troops accompanied by 40,000 Polish troops and 20,000 Polish Cavalry raced from the forest. Under the storied and brilliant leadership of King Sobieski, they flooded down the hills like a massive wave, raging through the enemy encampment and sweeping into the beleaguered city.

The new attacking forces took full advantage of glaring military miscalculations by the Turkish invaders. The tide of battle turned immediately. Hemmed in by a force of size equal to their own and cut off from their supplies, the Turks fled.

In their flight, the huge Turkish army left behind everything, beating a hasty retreat eastward toward the safety of the Ottoman Empire. Kara Mustafa paid dearly for his failure. Later arrested in Eastern Europe, he was stripped of his office and rank. Due to his insolence and inept leadership, he was executed by order of the sultan; his head presented to the sultan on a silver platter.

The victors proceeded to divide among themselves the massive hoard of provisions abandoned by the 140,000 invaders. Arsenals of weapons, storehouses of food, hundreds of wagons and seemingly endless supplies, including thousands and thousands of large bags packed with dried Arabic seeds. Unfamiliar with Turkish foodstuffs and finding no use for them, the Bavarians deemed them worthless and set to burning the mountainous bags of hard beans with the other piles of trash.

As for Kulcyzcki, brought before King Sobieski and the Bavarian rulers, his heroism met with great acclaim and gratitude. For such bravery and for saving the city, the rulers gave him the ultimate gift…they told him to name his prize. *Anything* he wished for would be his. A palace, a knighthood, a position in the king's courts…anything he wanted.

Kulcyzcki thought for a moment; then made his request. He asked to be given all of the remaining thousands of bags filled with the inexplicable seeds. Royal command immediately granted his simple request, and further rewarded him with a prominent location in the liberated city to conduct a business.

Within a few short years, his little Vienna-based business soon took the continent by storm. Jerzy Kulcyzcki became one of the most influential and wealthiest men in Europe.

For while infiltrating through the Turkish lines of 140, 000 men, he had taken the time to stop, to chat, to eat, and to drink, and he noted that what he drank appeared to be the resounding choice of everyone as far as the eye could see. Endlessly, and with enthusiasm, they drank of a rich, deep, dark brew made from the little, black beans…Turkish coffee.

By adding other exotic flavorings of the time such as sugar and chocolate to the mixture, he introduced all of Europe to the new, brewed drink. The toast of the continent immediately became renowned as "Vienna coffee", courtesy of Kulcyzcki.

Kulcyzcki succeeded where the Turks failed. He conquered all of Europe for all time. And a welcome conquest it was indeed. Just ask any coffee drinker.

Lasting rewards are not always found in a lofty station, an immediate prize or a high profile gift. The Polish mercenary might have enjoyed a few years of fading glory with an official post or grand possession that represented an "old trophy" or "wilting laurels".

Instead of selecting the obvious, he chose the leftovers as reward. Combining them with industriousness and vision, he gained lifelong success and widespread fame. Today, the entire world enjoys his choice.

The true reward may not be the obvious, but the path to something much greater; if you make it work.

26
The Impossible Possible
March 17, 1904 C.E.

In unison the standing room only crowd at the London Hippodrome ceased their chatter. Every head swiveled spellbound toward the front of the theatre. A lone figure emerged from a large, stark, black box that sat solitary upon the expansive stage. The rapt attention of this Edwardian crowd focused upon the most illustrious, famous magician and escape artist of modern times, Harry Houdini. Throughout the elegant theater, stunned silence had fallen upon the finely dressed audience of 4,000.

But at this instant…could this be the moment that the celebrated Harry Houdini finally failed to free himself? Had this challenge been more than he anticipated? Had he given up?

A sweltering heat gripped London on that St. Patrick's Day evening of March 17, 1904 as the great Houdini met the much publicized challenge to escape from the strongest, most complex hand restraints ever devised.

Houdini had accepted the challenge to attempt an escape from the legendary "Mirror Cuffs". It had taken a Birmingham blacksmith five years to build the encumbrances, which featured an impossible-to-pick nesting Bramah locks. They featured six sets of unique, complicated locks involving nine tumblers each. Every expert who examined them proclaimed they had never witnessed anything so complex. Authorities surmised this intricacy would be the final word in defeating the legendary escape artist. The 30 daily newspapers in London headlined and screamed the challenge to the public for weeks.

The now encompassing quiet of the vast theater only served to amplify the obvious; the celebrated escape artist appeared to be experiencing considerable trouble. The immense shackles still bound his wrists. Having been in the stage box for a considerable span of 35 minutes, he had emerged drenched in sweat. Troubled murmurs rippled and raced through the crowd.

Earlier the crowd had watched enamored as a committee of authorities frisked and searched Houdini for special lock-picking gadgets or unusual contrivances. Left with his formal suit and a couple of minor knickknacks that would serve no purpose, the judges stood convinced.

Satisfied that he concealed nothing of the sort to assist him, they secured the handcuffs firmly around Houdini's wrists. The magician then entered a barren, black stage box he dubbed his "Ghost House" that had also been thoroughly searched and inspected. The long minutes of waiting and wondering dragged endlessly. The crowd whispered quietly and sparsely at first, but they grew increasingly louder, more speculative, more widespread, and more doubtful of Houdini's abilities.

Then came his emergence from the box. The shackles still bound him. Was the Great Houdini surrendering in defeat? They crowd waited, holding a collective breath.

Showing no concern or stress over the shackles, Houdini calmly and politely asked if the handcuffs might be detached momentarily so that he could remove his coat since the evening remained exceedingly hot and humid. The blustery experts harrumphed and staunchly refused, believing the request to be a ruse to study the cuff locks' operation. The audience murmured a mixed reaction of agreement with the experts, while others held sympathy for the famous performer.

Being a consummate showman and a gentleman, Houdini bowed to the judges, tranquilly acknowledging the denial of his request. The performer then quietly moved toward center stage. Unruffled and without using his hands, he began a slow, rhythmic, completely orchestrated contortion, systematically working the buttoned coat up over his shoulders, above his head, then down and out to the ends of his arms. Once accomplishing this feat, Houdini began a second set of tightly controlled movements, shifting, scrunching, and curling himself up to obtain a small penknife in his vest pocket. Extracting it with his teeth, he carefully opened the small blade with his mouth. He maneuvered the knife about, positioning it with a practiced skill. Using twists and turns of his head and neck, gripping the knife with his teeth and tongue, Houdini commenced. He methodically slashed away at the garment until finally it fell in shambles to the floor, completely cut away from his body.

Four thousand people leaped to their feet screaming and cheering in delight, astonishment and admiration! Houdini gratefully acknowledged their applause, and then returned to the confines of the black cabinet. Now leaving the crowd abuzz with renewed confidence about his skills, Houdini spent another 35 minutes in his box. After a total of one hour and ten minutes, he emerged once again, unflustered and unfettered. Holding the open cuffs high above his head, Houdini was met with the deafening acclaim of a hero's triumph. The crowd converged on the stage, hoisted him up on their shoulders and carried him off to parade him in triumph in the streets of London.

In the press afterwards, the attending experts acknowledged their later realization that Houdini had been toying with them all along; that he possessed the incredible ability to escape the manacles in seconds. He simply provided everyone, including them, the heightened uncertainty, anticipation and excitement of the exploit. Houdini had once again lived up to his trademark slogan: "The Impossible Possible."

Harry Houdini, remembered as the world's most incredible magician, benchmarks the enduring standard by which all others since are measured. However his dazzling spectacles derived little from the supernatural. Hard work, endless practice, and constant conditioning constituted the core of Houdini's magic. Continuous research on all aspects of his profession comprised the ingredients of his mystery and unrivalled successes.

Mysteries may have appeared spontaneously solved, but Harry Houdini left nothing to chance. He prepared his body, his mind, his intellect, his spirit, his courage for each escapade, trick, performance and illusion. It was expertise and craft that built the tools of his trade. Houdini proved so coolly capable with each situation that his feats appeared supernatural to ordinary people.

Magic? Far less from luck, far more from preparation, if someone consistently performs the impossible, chances are the "Magic" derives from practice, discipline, and hard earned experience.

Being prepared makes the impossible... possible.

27
Demand and Supply
Circa 210 C.E.

Branded a spy and a traitor!

A young Chinese military leader, Zhuge Liang stepped out of his commanding officer's tent into absolute hopelessness. On the eve of a major river battle, Liang found that rival officers within his own camp had convinced the commanding general that the young leader was a spy, a traitor and a saboteur. They persuaded the commander that Liang had schemed to create a short supply of arrows so that his assigned troops would soon run out and stand helpless against the enemy. Liang, they asserted, was actually in league with the enemy, aiding them by setting up his own side for defeat.

     The seeds were sown but the old commander would not accept testimony alone toward condemnation. Being from an old, traditional school of military philosophy, he deemed that a test would reveal Liang's true allegiance. A trial by ordeal could exonerate him. If Liang failed, his execution would be swift and certain.

     The young leader was given only one option for survival. He had to prove his allegiance by tilting the scales of advantage for the battle back to his kingdom. The request seemed simple, yet absolutely impossible: supply his troops with 100,000 arrows by the next day or instead be executed as a spy and traitor.

     Emerging from his commander's tent Liang must have believed his entire world had collapsed. Betrayed and condemned by his leader and comrades, he found himself burdened with an unachievable task that equaled his death sentence. Everyone and everything stood against him. Given the depth of betrayal and sheer hopelessness of the task, Bitterness, Blame and Helplessness reached for and clutched at Liang, encouraging resignment to fate's cruel twist. What choice had he? Obviously the division of soldiers under his command could not produce the vast volume of arrows required.

     Liang made his decision. He rebuffed the emotions that would forfeit his focus to handle the task at hand. He discarded the inducement to yield to his enemies' conspiracy. Instead he pressed his mind for possibilities and options. Then he set about formulating a plan…

Early on the morn of the anticipated battle while the fog and mist still hung thickly over the water, Liang took a trusted group of men far upriver with a dozen, large boats. He then ordered the men to tether the boats together and directed them to cover the barges with thick straw bales. Liang released the flotilla to float down the river. The current would do the rest.

Through the heavy haze enemy sentries suddenly sighted the invading boats. The alarm was sounded! In short order rank upon rank; hundreds and hundreds of archers lined up along the river bank. The signal was given. Volley after volley of arrows rained down upon the boats as they passed. Believing the ships to be the advance assault of Liang's troops, the barrage of arrows continued unabated for many long minutes. The boats never approached the shore but by the time they had floated down river and beyond the enemy encampment, the hay bristled with a virtual forest of expended enemy arrows. Through the deep fog, the adversaries believed they had staved off an initial sneak attack, decimating the entire invading force.

In a singular stroke of genius, Liang supplied his general with the required 100,000 arrows. But he went well beyond the request. The young officer stripped his foe of that same store hold of ammunition. He furnished his opponents a false sense of victory, lowering their guard for later attack. In addition Liang obtained an accurate picture of their battle readiness and training, having forced his opposition to reveal their number, ranks and intended battlefield strategies.

Such a wealth of information proved invaluable to Liang's commander. Such loyalty could not be questioned. The young leader's determined response, insight and resourcefulness vastly impressed the general. Liang's critics, revealed for what they were…were silenced.

Liang had faced impossible circumstances brought about by the betrayal of his colleagues. The confrontation may have stricken, but did not stop him. It may be a familiar feeling, standing abandoned, alone and betrayed by ones' peers. A decision will be needed. The choice to resist succumbing to blame and emotion allows one to respond with a clear mind.

The one able to think clearly can create solutions…and overcome.

28
How You Say It
1882 C.E.

Flanking an infinite array of fine bone china plates and ornate solid-silver serving wares, rank upon rank of gleaming silverware lay regimented along the vast tables. An overhead galaxy of chandeliers illuminates the immense room burgeoning with extravagant opulence. Forests of sterling silver candlesticks lavish a warm elegant glow amongst the sumptuous festivities. Immersed in this grand extravaganza, the formally dressed assembly of notable names and personalities of the era gathered to feast and hob-nob. Rows of liveried waiters deliver courses of exotic gourmet offerings for the rich and powerful in business, government and society.

Later, vintage liqueurs and wines flowed. The timbre of fine fluted glasses mixed with privileged conversations involving high society, business transactions, political ambitions and the latest fashions in Europe. Suddenly and impulsively the host brought the attention of the assembled high profile luminaries and sophisticates to himself and made an introduction. He noted that in this gilded age following the Civil War, there reigned few great ladies of the dramatic stage. Fewer still to make such memorable impact with her spellbinding stagecraft as renowned Polish actress, Lady Helena Modjeska, beloved and admired on both sides of the Atlantic; hailed the greatest female Shakespearian player of the Victorian age.

Bowing deeply to the famed actress sitting in their presence that night, the host completed his glowing accolades, thanking Lady Modjeska for the honor of her company. He then beseeched her to share with them a presentation of her renowned dramatic talent.

All eyes turned with great anticipation toward the surprised actress. Perhaps a slight reluctance fluttered across her gaze, yet any excuse to bow out would be improper among such fine company. Instead the consummate actress smiled, calmly stood and gazed upon her rapt audience. Stepping to the forefront and extending the sweep of her elegant floor length gown, Lady Helena Modjeska launched into a compelling, captivating performance.

With her very first utterance Helena took command of her immediately enthralled listeners. She accompanied her powerful vocal delivery with expressive gestures. Her eyes flashed, her voice and face reflected myriad expressions. Fascination flowed into fury, abject distress careened into sheer joy. Helena alternately beckoned and dismissed the audience as she eloquently held them spellbound. She intertwined deep heartfelt expressions and gestures with a touching, enrapturing voice. Though she recited in her native Polish tongue the gathered listeners sat, ardently immersed in her fervent recitation. By the time Lady Modjeska ceased her gripping presentation, and although no one had understood the words of her Polish language, her listeners sat stunned, emotionally drained and many brought to tears by her stirring performance.

To those listening, the recitation reiterated her prestigious reputation and the kudos their host had bestowed upon her earlier. Only much later was it revealed that Helena's outstanding, spontaneous performance drawing the heart-wrenching sentiment, and ardent audience admiration resulted from her simple but skillful narration of the Polish alphabet.

Helena conveyed a message with great emotion without language. The spoken word accounts for only seven percent of what a listener assimilates. The overwhelming majority of all communication a person perceives and interprets emerges from posture, tone, gestures and facial expressions.

At ninety-three percent, our body language and vocal inflection articulate, reveal and influence far more than our discourse...as proven by Helena Modjeska. Lady Modjeska's words, superfluous; how she said them...brought down the house.

Actions do speak louder than words. In life, when our actions match our words, the message emerges...and is received, far more powerfully than one can imagine.

29
Sequoia Secrets

The giant Sequoia trees stand alone as the largest living things on Earth. Indeed on the entire planet the Sequoias stand not only as the largest, but also among the most ancient. These majestic trees grow naturally only on the western slope of the Sierra Nevada mountain range in California. They tower up to 300 feet, as tall as the length of a football field. The trees can reach 100 feet in diameter, far surpassing half the width of a football field. Sequoias seem almost immortal. The oldest known Sequoia lived 3,200 years. There exist living specimens as aged as 2,700 years; dating back to 700 BCE. Envision a living thing that existed over half millennia before Jesus Christ, prior to the birth of the Roman Empire and has eclipsed all subsequent rulers, empires, kingdoms, nations and world cataclysms that have passed through the ages since.

Even when standing dwarfed by their presence, as one's gaze is swept upward to the skies in utter, overwhelming awe, it still remains difficult to comprehend the immense size, extreme age and monumental stature of the Sequoia trees.

Stately, commanding, antiquated; the Sequoias' survival secrets lie deep within their great, tall forests. With their slow combustible sap, these trees can survive fast-moving forest fires. Pestilence is daunted by the high tannin content in their wood and bark. Bugs and fungi find it distasteful, plus it assists in healing the trees from disease and damage. As well, the brittle consistency of the Sequoias' wood renders it useless for building, making it undesirable to mankind.

Yet as old, massive and impervious as the Sequoias are, they possess a very shallow root system, and no taproot to anchor them. Beneath the ground, the formidable Sequoias are exceptionally frail and highly vulnerable, subject to toppling. Falling ranks as the nearly exclusive threat to their quest for immortality. Any number of natural elements can easily fell the great trees. Strong winds or root damage combined with drought, soil erosion, or excessive water as rain or flood can bring them down with ease.

But the Sequoias harbor an unseen secret to their extended survival. They only grow in groves, allowing their shallow roots to intricately intertwine with the other trees around them and throughout the grove. Supporting each other, the foundation of community provides the Sequoia its longevity and strength through life's buffetings.

When storms arise, threatening to topple us, when our roots are too shallow to hold on, it is the interweaving in our relationships that can help to hold us up and carry on.

Beginning at our roots and reaching to the tallest points that any of us might aspire, let us fully appreciate and nurture the depth of our relationships with each other. If we devote ourselves to it, then like the Sequoias, the world eventually may one day stand in awe of what we stand for and how we grew...together.

30
Posthumous Hero
April 1943

In the 1940's they branded such an individual a fop, a "ne'er-do-well", a member of the idle-rich class. This particular reveling fellow happened to be in his late twenties, completely irresponsible, mildly handsome, and a carousing drunk known for often getting himself into various problems. His last bit of trouble cost him dearly however. After a rousing bout of heavy drinking, he staggered out and onto the London streets alone, but didn't quite make it home. Passed-out drunk, he spent the night on the street completely unguarded amidst the biting cold and the dank, damp fog. In early April 1943, he developed pneumonia and died.

Shortly thereafter he was drafted by the British Army, immediately promoted to the rank of Major and dispatched on a Top Secret mission against the Nazis.

And he completed his perilous mission successfully.

It comprised a bold and simple plan put forth by two bright British military chaps named Emmet and Archibald whose top secret wartime post consisted of coming up with…well, bold and simple plans.

This new strategy involved the highly important, very secret, Allied invasion of the Italian island of Sicily. The Nazis and Italian Fascists knew the offensive loomed on the horizon and had prepared superbly for it. The Allies knew the Nazis knew but wanted them to believe they knew more than they actually knew.

Our hero, the recently dead and freshly promoted British Major, found the entire mission of misdirecting the enemy resting upon his broad shoulders, dependent upon his unwavering, fearless approach to his duties. The new Major himself would be personally dispatched to deliver the Allies' Top Secret Invasion Plans…to the Spanish.

In the pre-dawn darkness on the morning of April 20, 1943, a submarine surfaced a couple of miles off the coast of Spain. Seamen struggled mightily to bring a massively heavy, hugely oversized, oddly oblong crate through the hatch and up on deck. Then with a short prayer and a quick salute, the crate's contents tumbled into the sea; a body kept "fresh and frozen" within the heavy box packed full of ice.

Our Hero, reporting for duty.

He washed ashore late that day. Churning amidst the shoreline tides, he was soon spotted by the Spanish beachcombers who waded out to rescue him. They took him at face value, the victim of a plane crash at sea. His aviators' helmet, goggles and life vest attested to that fact. He obviously appeared to be a smart, handsome British officer of importance and rank. His uniform indicated his war record. Spain being a neutral country in World War II, would handle such a situation differently than an active combatant. The beachcombers dutifully called in the local law enforcement who also took our Major at face value.

Of course as anticipated, the Spanish authorities quietly and immediately contacted their friends, the Nazis.

The Germans looked beyond face value, bringing far greater suspicion and scrutiny. They thoroughly investigated. The Major had the usual military ID and insignia on the uniform. His pockets told his story. There existed a multitude of personal items: a wallet with theater ticket stubs, a receipt for an engagement ring, love letters from his girl, a pair of dice, pocket change, a small amount of paper money in the wallet. There were pictures of family, his fiancé, a letter from his father, and even some unpaid bills for lodging and meals. His information checked out, right down to his military assignment. He obviously crashed at sea and drowned.

And then there was the briefcase. Yes, there happened to be this rather conspicuous, diplomatic courier style metal briefcase securely handcuffed to his wrist. It sported dual locks…must be very important items tucked away in there.

But it could all be a fake. The crafty Germans were still not convinced…not entirely. They ordered an autopsy. Once they opened the corpse up, the results were conclusive: he had fluid in his lungs. He had definitely drowned. But they did not check the fluid to determine if it was sea water…or the results of pneumonia. The presence of liquid convinced them of his authenticity. Sharp attention therefore turned to the briefcase. Within were the top-secret invasion plans. Since the corpse proved real, then logically, the plans must be real.

The next day, the Spanish authorities contacted the English, sadly informing them that a young British army airman had perished at sea and had been recovered by them. Due to the restrictions of the war, they afforded him an excellent burial with full military honors in Spain. His belongings were sent home for the family. And among the items sat an attaché case. It appeared untouched.

Lab testing however revealed the locks had been very carefully tampered with and opened; the contents had been thoroughly photographed.

As a result, when the British did invade Sicily as planned shortly thereafter, the Nazis did not realize it until most of the island had been overrun. The superbly prepped defenses of the Germans had shifted to the other side of the island where the attack supposedly should have occurred…based on the top-secret information obtained from a certain, dead English Major. The man who never was had performed his mission superbly and ended things a true hero.

Occasionally there exists a feeling that life has passed without one having contributed to it. Nothing attained, no legacy left behind. Our fop's accomplishment might alter this outlook. One should never assume that they have been of no consequence in life…or beyond it. So be prepared for one never knows when opportunity may arise.

31
The Right Word
1934 C.E.

By the mid 1930's, lionized Irish dramatist, George Bernard Shaw towered as the leading figurehead in 20th Century theater. Self educated through extraordinary amounts of time spent studying every subject imaginable at the British Museum, his thought provoking scripts with social commentary and razor-sharp wit raised him to prestigious standing. Socialist spokesman, freethinker, defender of women's rights, advocate of income equality, literary critic and playwright who spoke beyond common themes, Shaw's comments and visage appeared for innumerable issues and causes. Awarded the Nobel Prize for Literature in 1925, Shaw shocked the world by accepting the honor but refusing the money.

During the midst of his ever-increasing popularity, Shaw received an unusual letter from a somewhat eccentric New York socialite. She wrote:

"Dear Mr. Shaw,
I recently read with interest a news article in which a statistician compiled all the words collected from your various literary works and divided it by the gross receipts and royalties you have gained. He estimated that in your career, you have averaged $5.00 for every word you have written."

Considering this time period of the 1930's Great Depression, the amount mentioned would be a considerable sum of money. Well-paid bank tellers earned $5.00 for an entire week's salary. However, the complimenting letter then took a strange twist...

"Enclosed is $5.00...
Please send me one of your words."

To a famous celebrity like Shaw, such a letter could be ignored or considered a prank. A busy man, and not one to dawdle in folly, one could question if Shaw would take the missive seriously enough to compose a genuine response.

He did. Nearly a month later, the New York woman received an envelope from Shaw. Inside was a neatly folded, single piece of stationary. A single word appeared upon it:

"Thanks."

Newspapers regaled his response. The innocuous and insignificant incident generated tremendous publicity for Shaw. And the socialite certainly received her money's worth through attention in high society columns and the local news sections of the papers.

Shaw, a person whose fame rested upon a superior command of language, created a rejoinder that proved appropriate, exacting, well thought, and humorous. One word revealed the precision, thought and wit that Shaw infused with the use of a single, simple word.

If a man so renowned regarding his use of words would choose one so carefully, how much more should we?

32
Monstrous Opportunity
1931 C.E.

William Pratt sat quietly amidst the hustle and bustle of the noisy movie studio commissary. Once again he ran his fingers over the words on the paper before him just to make certain it was true. He was realizing every actor's dream...he had gotten the part!

Like most aspiring actors, William's deep desire had kept him pursuing the dream. He had spent much of the last decade as a truck driver for a lumber company, mundane employment while he chased his ambition. With gaunt facial features that projected a penetrating, hardened appearance, there had been a few small gangster parts for him. However major acting jobs remained illusive. After all, Hollywood from the start had gloried in youth and beauty. William didn't fit that role. But now after 20 years of performing in small theater plays, stand-in parts and bit pieces, William Pratt had finally landed a major role. The memo was even personally signed by James Whale, noted Hollywood director. Here was the opportunity of a lifetime!

However the initial thrill paled quickly. Although Pratt would have substantial screen time with major actors, he found his character to be considered extremely minor, mere window dressing to enhance the real stars. Still he figured his acting and vocal ability should boost his celebrity status. As he read the screenplay he abruptly understood his role amounted to a little more than a lumbering, mute monster. Pratt's distinctive voice would be lost in scripted utterances that consisted of a few guttural grunts and growls.

Upon arriving at the set William thought that with his extensive screen time, audiences would at least recognize his face. But talented make up artist, James Pierce, had created a cumbersome prosthetic that not only extended William's head, it also flattened and squared it beyond human appearance. Embalmer's wax leaded down Pratt's eyelids, sealing off his hope to beguile through eye contact. Heavy pancake make up, layers upon layers of it, plastered William's face, nullifying expression.

There seemed no end to the impediments and hindrances. Left with little else, William hoped that moviegoers might discern and recognize a skill and talent they could admire in his physical performance. Then he saw his costume. Nearly 50 pounds in weight, it

100

featured a five-pound spinal brace that not only stiffened his spine, but also effectively halted the movement in his arms and legs. His feet were encased in high platformed, asphalt-spreader boots, weighing an overbearing 12 pounds each. A padded body suit to lend bulk, and a coat with the sleeves cut too short finished the outfit.

After being shackled into this get-up along with the grotesque cosmetics, William found himself transformed into an immobilized, speechless and unrecognizable "thing." Worse yet, he had no clue if his character appeared scary or laughable. Stepping outside the make up room to practice walking in the brace, William suddenly confronted a prop master who had hurriedly rounded the corner of the building. The prop master stopped, staring face to face with William. Both men just stood there and said nothing …then the prop man gulped in terror, turned and fled, never to be seen on the lot again. This was Pratt's "Big Break"?

William still sought potential with the tools he had been provided: extensive screen time, grunts and growls, a terrifying appearance and stilted limitations in movement…and he made it work in his favor. Despite the drawbacks and restrictions, he crafted each element with talent and ability to create a unique character, eliciting intense fear mixed with sympathy. He gave the role his best shot.

Even so the challenges continued. In post production on this black and white film, the special effects department hand painted a sickening green pallor to heighten the horror in every on-screen image of Pratt's character. In the film credits, his performance was considered so minor that the studio simply billed him with a question mark: *"? – as the Monster."* The movie executives had so little expectation for William's part in the film they didn't even bother signing him to a contract.

By the end of the first showing of the film, the Hollywood moguls were more shocked and terrified than the frightened and screaming audience. It was apparent immediately that the crowd could not care less about the big name stars because they were absolutely entranced with the nameless monster.

The executives scrambled to sign William Pratt with a long-term contract. Even buried in the bulky monster outfit, he genuinely represented true talent.

And if you were wondering, the name of the film that this "minor character" completely overwhelmed…

Frankenstein

101

From that moment in 1931 and over the next 38 years of his life…even continuing after death to this present day, this gentleman of class and kindness, William Pratt, will always be remembered as one of the true legends of Hollywood. Of course, a name like William Henry Pratt is not very exotic or evocative of the Hollywood mystique, so he changed it to Boris Karloff.

Everyday opportunities come to us in many shapes and manners. Sometimes like the role of Frankenstein's monster, they appear so overburdened or stifling that they hardly resemble prospects at all. But as Boris Karloff exemplified, it is not the opportunity…it is what we <u>do</u> with the opportunity that counts.

There are monstrous potentials and possibilities to be seized in every opportunity that comes each day.

33
Unforeseen Circumstance
March 15, 44 B.C.E,

The sun beamed broadly overhead that bright morning in 44 BCE. Gaius Julius Caesar stood confidently on his palace balcony and surveyed a great city and a vast empire that was his alone to command. On this day in particular, his victor's self-assurance overflowed. He, Gaius Julius, the great Caesar, the highly respected, the most famous, and the all-powerful, had lived through the previous night, and continued to rule the known world.

For some time previous, Julius had found himself troubled, even fearful. Dark premonitions had clouded the horizon. His people, the highly superstitious Romans, perceived even minor incidents, accidents and ironies as warnings of Fate. The direction the birds flew or the way the wind blew was interpreted with divination. Whether he believed in foretelling or not, the widespread recent months' reports of various omens portending Caesar's demise had been unnerving.

Recent demolition in a centuries-old tomb unearthed a cryptic hand-written message predicting a great leader's demise at the hands of friends. The torment lay with the eerie revelation that the deceased in the tomb proved a forbearer to Gaius Julius, his distant relative. Along the Rubicon River, the hundreds of captive horses Caesar had earlier freed in a glorious dedication to the river god Rubico as gratitude for Julius' famous defeat of his enemy Pompey began to rail and storm about chaotically. The agitated steeds, unstoppable, inconsolable, neighing and crying with anxiety, led to rumors alleging distress regarding their liberator... Julius Caesar. Finally, while Caesar himself waded through the adulating crowds several weeks earlier, Spurinna, a wizened old soothsayer had broken through the well-wishing throngs and coldly confronted Julius. "Beware the Ides of March!" the seer icily foretold.

Perhaps the boldness or manner of the prediction struck Caesar, but the final prophecy had chilled him to the core as nothing ever had. Fear and suspicion haunted his waking hours. He initiated numerous inquiries among his compatriots, seeking assurance that no plots against him existed. His trusted aids, closest associates and dearest friends worked to bolster Julius' confidence, dismissing the ominous forewarnings. And each evening Julius watched for the Ides with increasing apprehension as the moon increasingly commandeered the night sky.

Rather than identify individual days as Monday through Sunday, ancient calendars grouped days, and named them according to the phases of the moon. The Ides represented the arrival of the fullest point of the moon in its monthly cycle; the early morning hours when the completed moon reached its zenith in the night sky before beginning its downward wane. For the mighty Caesar, the forecast appointment with the Ides of March, and his doom had now passed with the apex of the full moon. The omens and charlatans proved false. Julius greeted the new day with verve; he had not been murdered in the weeks prior, or during the Ides that March night.

Julius now viewed the whole episode as amounting to nothing but superstition. And as usual, he, Gaius Julius, had confronted it and overcome. From the very start his life had been one of challenge. A survivor of a violent birth, ripped from his mother's womb, the procedure to this day is dubbed a "Caesarian Section" or "C-Section" birth. In Rome's army, Julius time and again proved his mettle, facing enemies of the Roman Empire in bloody battles. Rising to general, Julius marched his forces to the farthest regions of the known world. In strange and fearful lands, against fierce foes, Gaius Julius met challenge and overcame it. Julius dared break rank with stringent military rules and engaged in a torrid love affair with the clever Cleopatra, who assisted him in his conquest of Egypt. He brought distant new lands under the empire's dominion, providing Rome its greatest expansions to date.

By 49 BCE, Gaius Julius emerged the survivor through several escalating, political and military campaigns to oust him from his increasingly powerful roles. Facing either annihilation or national exile, he risked everything, committing his army to a full conflict with his own homeland. Upon defeating Pompey, the last of his rivals, Julius sent word to Rome in a timeless catchphrase for success: Veni, Vedi, Vici – I came, I saw, I conquered.

The vast popularity and immense success of the man with the citizens of Rome gave the powerful Roman Senate no choice. Begrudgingly, they were forced to proclaim him CAESAR, "Emperor of the Empire", and dictator for life. The first Latin word utilized across the Teutonic languages, Caesar's title arcs across the centuries as the designation for the ensuing rulers of ancient Rome and into modern times as Kaiser in the Holy Roman Empire, Austria and Germany and Czar in Russia.

And now, with Fate and the heavens having also plotted against him, Gaius Julius Caesar once again emerges victorious. The proof: self-evident. The spectral full moon had arrived the night before. He had survived and believed he now had nothing to fear from some false prophet in the market place.

Preparing himself for a busy day at the senate, the Emperor of Rome relished in every aspect of the morning. He took his time. Having donned his most regal attire, he strode confidently through the streets. The crowds gathered to cheer him as always, yet to Caesar today their hoopla carried stronger applause of approval and adoration.

Nearing the government buildings around mid morning, Caesar stopped then turned to take a different route to the senate edifice. Scanning the multitudes, he finally observed the object of his search. Boldly confronting the soothsayer, Julius Caesar straightened to his full height, full supremacy, full grandeur.

"The Ides of March has arrived!" he proclaimed with great gusto, gesturing expansively to himself, his vigor and appearance.

Spurinna paused momentarily, looked up at the emperor and smiled disquietly.

"Indeed it has," the seer replied cryptically, "but it is not yet passed."

Within the hour, sixty members of the senate would convene, and then violently converge on Julius Caesar. The death proved legendary; a tale still told to this day. Receiving 23 vicious stab wounds from various attackers including his closest friends, Julius Caesar's reputed final words pursed a sad question. Facing his final assailant, his devoted comrade, Brutus, he asked… "Et tu, Brutus?" …and you also, Brutus?

Julius Caesar, the most powerful man on earth, died alone in a bloody heap on the open floor of the senate building. He lay crumpled in the center of the capital of the known world, forlorn and deceased for two hours before three of his slaves dared finally to remove him.

According to historians, far more than any superstitious signs revealed trouble had been brewing, but Gaius Julius Caesar had relaxed his guard based on time and omens rather than circumstances.

A situation confronted does not mean that it has passed.

34
Contents of the Lunch Bucket
July, 2002 C.E

The place: a coal mine in central Pennsylvania ~ July, 2002. The event: two hundred and forty feet below ground in a cramped, four-foot high mining tunnel where a team of nine soot-covered miners digs for coal. According to the engineering maps, a similar mine, abandoned half a century earlier and now flooded with ground water, lay a goodly 300 yards away.

The map and engineers grossly miscalculated. The continued digging suddenly fractured a wall separating the two mines. In an instant the ruptured old mine began unleashing a torrential fifty million gallons of frigid, fifty-five degree ground water into the active mine with the men. It happened so fast. Nine miners at the breach point had ten seconds to scramble in the dark against the icy, violent flood rapidly filling the four foot high tunnel. Desperately they attempted to attain an exit shaft. They didn't make it. Trapped. Ten seconds transformed into a terror filled, 77 hour, life and death ordeal.

As escape quickly proved fruitless, one of the men immediately radioed another group of miners warning them of the surging floodwaters. That second group, saved by the frantic call, escaped unharmed and quickly joined the rescue team.

Nine men. They crouch, trapped two hundred and forty feet beneath the earth in a cave swirling with rising, ice cold water; enveloped in pitch black with a ceiling only four feet high. Caught in between...can't stand up, can't sit down. It's very dank and dark. It's very cold.

The freezing waters continued to rise--nearly to their noses. Painful cold and dampness invaded their bodies and spirits. Hours and hours passed. Their joints ached. Hands and feet became numb. Between themselves, they held onto hope. And they made a systematic plan:

- They huddled together to keep each other warm.
- They moved each other's arms and legs to stimulate circulation.
- They calmed each other so no one would have a heart attack through the combination of stress and the icy water.

- They found a narrow ledge that enabled them to keep their faces above water.
- They shared a corned beef sandwich, a Pepsi, and two cans of Mountain Dew from a lunch pail that happened to float by their perch.
- They tethered themselves to one another so if they didn't survive, their bodies would be found together.
- They struggled to write final letters to their loved ones; their last private thoughts. Placing them in the lunch bucket, they sealed it.
- They prayed for deliverance.

Teamwork. Nine men working together and the creation of a fierce, loyal camaraderie, supporting each other hour after hour while facing an increasingly certain end.

Two hundred and forty feet above them, the rescue team worked feverishly as time rapidly slipped away. Surveyors quickly guesstimated where the men may be. They guessed right. Rescuers drilled a six-inch air hole and pumped hot air into the cavern, hoping to aid the men somewhat. Dozens of pumps set to work removing water from the mine as quickly as possible. Rescuers brought in heavy equipment and started boring a three-foot wide rescue shaft, but the over-sized drill bit broke 130 feet down. Such large, drilling attachments are highly uncommon. The nearest replacement was located in Ohio, a state away. With desperation, that drill bit was rushed to the site, but the distance and delays ripped precious hours from the rescue window. Anxiously, drilling finally resumed on the rescue shaft. After 77 hours – over three days of intense, constant work and tense, fearful waiting above and below ground, the men were reached. One by one each emerged to safety.

The nine miners survived together with minimal physical injuries. People felt the blessings of the Almighty had enveloped the miners and the rescue team. Everyone was immensely thankful.

And doubts? Were there doubts among the minors trapped in such a grim situation? Undoubtedly. And at their greatest moment of uncertainty, they each took scraps of paper and expended time to privately write down their final thoughts…words shadowed in the belief that failure and death would soon grip each of them. They then sealed these deeply personal doubts, feelings and thoughts inside a lunch box that had come drifting along.

Following their harrowing episode and rescue, the nine minors have vowed that they will never open the lunch bucket.

107

That may seem a very good idea. Write down one's regrets and deepest feelings, and pack them away; to have a place to leave doubts whenever courage, determination and faith are needed. However like the minors' closed lunch box, our own internal "lunchbox" also remains...still holding those doubts and misgivings carefully sequestered inside. Each time it is seen; there will be a reminder of what forebodings it holds. It seals them up, but also never releases them...and only serves as a reminder they remain unresolved.

Take the time to unseal that lunch box, confront, overcome and vanquish those doubts from life.

And leave the box empty.

35
Take Note
July 10-11, 1969 C.E.

Five hundred million people, one fifth of the entire population of the earth, hovered transfixed in awe at the gray, fuzzy images flickering on every television screen, on every channel. By far the largest television audience in history, family and friends everywhere gathered to stare, waiting for days, hour upon hour before anything transpired. Millions attempted to photograph family members in front of their television screens, hoping to capture the image for themselves forever. Those unable to witness the experience on TV waited by radios, captivated, listening intently to the step by step descriptions shared by the giants of world media and the scientific community. Others without TV or radio peered deeply into the night sky, seeking to plumb the depths and comprehend the moment, the distance, and the monumental event of human history occurring far off in the heavens.

Dusty boot prints on the lunar landscape left an indelible imprint on hearts, minds and imaginations around the globe. Occurring in their lifetime from 240,000 miles away, people the world over watched and listened. Every minute of the mission was meticulously documented. No other single adventure had ever been shared by more people; no individual quest had ever given more hope to the potential of human determination and technology. Spanning a mere 67 years, powered flight had transcended from a rickety, homespun creation barely capable to lift one man a scant few feet into the air over several shaky seconds to this colossal accomplishment, landing on the moon.

And like that first flight at Kitty Hawk, etched with tension and trepidation, the lunar landing also flirted with danger at every turn. The computer-selected landing site turned out to be a crater strewn with boulders capable of toppling the *Eagle* lunar landing module. With only 114 seconds of fuel left, the astronauts overrode the computer-controlled landing program to quickly seek a level spot, or face aborting the entire, long awaited mission of man landing on the moon. As the moment of truth occurred, it felt as if the whole world held its breath July 10, 1969, to watch Americans Neil Armstrong and Edwin "Buzz" Aldrin successfully set down upon the moon at 102 hours, 45 minutes and 58 seconds into the mission.

"Tranquility base here. The *Eagle* has landed." called out Buzz as the Lunar Excursion Module settled gently amidst a puff of dust in a giant crater called the Sea of Tranquility.

"Roger, Tranquility. We copy you on the ground. You got a bunch of guys about to turn blue, we're breathing again, thank you." Houston responded at 102:46:06. Tears and cheers sang out at Mission Control and across the earth. Only thirty two seconds of fuel remained.

Following six hours of preparation and double checking equipment should any immediate mission abort be required, the cameras attached to the LEM were finally turned on and the two astronauts emerged from the *Eagle*. They stepped down the nine rungs of the landing module ladder. At 109:24:48 into the historic mission, Armstrong stepped off the ladder onto the lunar surface. His famous words, "That's one small step for man; one giant leap for mankind" echoed across the moon, the earth and history.

Among the masses glued to their TV sets sat a Los Angeles businessman named Paul Fisher, feeling proud with the rest of the world. A writing pen of his design had made the journey aboard the Apollo 11 spacecraft.

In the 1950's, Paul Fisher served as executive for a company producing the newly introduced and very expensive ball point pens; pens that frequently leaked and infrequently wrote. Appalled at the poor quality he was expected to represent, Fisher walked out on his very lucrative position as chief of sales and marketing. He initiated his own business and spent over a million dollars developing a dependable writing pen of which he could be proud. His stellar achievement, a sleek metal instrument, wrote in any extreme temperature, on any surface including wet paper, glass or metal, and from any conceivable angle. In 1965, NASA sought an efficient pen that would operate in the intense temperature fluctuations of space. Fisher sent his pen for consideration, and as they say, the rest is history. NASA purchased several hundred Fisher pens, sending a limited number on subsequent manned space flights. In his early efforts with his pens, Fisher had not foreseen his invention given such lofty assignment, but felt pleased he had contributed in the space program, particularly today as humanity stepped upon the surface of the moon.

For two and a half hours the people of planet earth united in watching and listening with awe as every aspect of the historic moment was broadcast live from the moon. Enthusiastically, Armstrong and

Aldrin reported all that they observed and experienced; completed requisite scientific experiments including the gathering of rock and soil samples, played at golf, and ceremoniously planted the American stars and stripes upon the surface of the moon. Of course, the excitement proved overwhelming, as Houston had to remind the talkative Armstrong several times to focus on the needed priority tasks, should they have to abort.

At 110:16:03, Mission Control in Houston, Texas, announced to the astronauts:

"The President of the United States is in his office now and would like to say a few words to you."

The spacemen heard the voice of President Nixon from 240,000 miles away.

"This certainly has to be the most historic telephone call ever made. ...for people all over the world I am sure they too join with Americans in recognizing what a feat this is... As you talk to us from the Sea of Tranquility, it inspires us to redouble our efforts to bring peace and tranquility to Earth. For one priceless moment, in the whole history of man, all the people on this Earth are truly one."

Ending their trek upon the moon, Armstrong and Aldrin performed one final task. They saluted the American flag they had planted with pride and left a plaque signed by President Nixon and the 3 astronauts of the Apollo 11 crew stating, "Here men from the planet earth first set foot upon the Moon July 1969 AD. We came in peace for all mankind." A memorial disk also remained, containing statements by leaders of 72 nations, Pope Paul VI and U.S. Presidents Eisenhower, Kennedy, Johnson and Nixon.

Too soon, the thrilling images were brought to a close as Mission Control ordered the astronauts return to the *Eagle* LEM to initiate preparations for their rendezvous with the mother ship, *Columbia*, orbiting the moon.

At 111:39:25 into the mission, Armstrong and Aldrin flipped the switch to shut down the exterior cameras that had been recording history to the planet earth. With even greater labor than it took exiting the Lander, the two men now climbed back up the nine steps of the ladder with forty pounds of dirt and rocks in tow. With great effort they squeezed jostled and crammed the samples and themselves back into the *Eagle*.

A brilliant work of engineering, every aspect of the landing module had been carefully planned out. The *Eagle* consisted of two pieces of equipment; a descent and an ascent stage. The descent section carried landing engines, the four leg base, storage area for equipment, the ladder the spacemen would use and the cameras for filming on the moon's surface. It also served as the launch platform for the ascent module.

In the ascent module not a single inch of wasted space or weight existed. Everything, including mountains of scientific equipment, mass arrays of navigational and piloting instruments, retro rockets, tanks of fuel, communications, life support and much more were precisely planned and placed; crammed into a compact vehicle that measured a precise exterior diameter of 13 feet by 12 feet. It managed to have just enough room for the two astronauts to stand side by side in their bulky space suits with life support packs, no seats at all. The area was so crowded there was no room to step around each other. When re-entering the module, both men knew Aldrin must enter first to be next to the flight control panels.

Perhaps the jammed interior compared to sardines being packed in a tin, but the LEM did offer welcome protection from the extreme lunar heat and cold. With no atmosphere to insulate, the moon's surface broils to 180 F when the sun basks upon it and quickly drops to an average of - 200 F in the absence of sunlight. Although both men were seriously cold and damp in their cumbersome space suits, being closed up in the *Eagle* would allow them to relinquish their oversized helmets and bulky life support packs. Two hours and thirty one minutes after they began, they shut and sealed the hatch to begin preparations for the departure and rendezvous. The moon walk had been a stellar success.

The earth celebrated

An incredible moment in history, the accolades came pouring in from around the world. Even the Foreign Minister of the Soviet Union, dreaded Cold War enemies and fierce competitors in the space race for two decades, sent a congratulatory telegram. Newspaper headlines and broadcasts around the globe touted the amazing news of the first man on the moon.

The Astronauts settled back in; exuberant, victorious, and finally able to shed their awkward life support gear. To lighten their craft for the return trip, they discarded all unneeded items such as tools, boots and other equipment, jettisoning it onto the lunar surface. An hour later, while coordinating final take off preparations, at 112:56:28 Aldrin suddenly asked an unusual question:

"Houston, Tranquility. Do you have a way of showing the configuration of the engine arm circuit breaker? Over." (Long pause)

"The reason I'm asking is because the end of it appears to be broken off."

There often exists a very fine thread betwixt triumph and tragedy. Within mere moments the euphoric and triumphant astronauts had crossed that diaphanous line.

The little plastic flip switch was not there. Earlier when observing unexpected moon dust scattered on the floor, Aldrin noted a small, broken twist of plastic that didn't belong. Now, he feared he had just discovered where it should have been.

No one knows, but it probably happened when the men had exited the snug lunar module. Likely Aldrin's huge and unwieldy life-support backpack brushed the control panel. Two switches were damaged. One mashed in; the other completely sheered off the control panel. And not just any switch. This toggle didn't link to mere light or minor gauges. This missing plastic piece happened to be the arming mechanism for firing the *Eagle*'s retro rockets; switching open the circuit that would send electrical power to the ascent engine for lift-off. This circuit, now inaccessible, was their only way off the moon...

In that moment of realization, their whole world stopped. A vacant hole in the panel belied the switch had once existed. The astronauts looked down the narrow hole to spy a tiny metal strip that must be bridged to connect the circuit and ignite the engine. Less than an inch away, it may as well have been on the next planet. No delicate repair could be accomplished. In additional effort to lighten the Lunar Module, nonrequisite tools had been left on *Columbia*.

Every aspect of the mission had been precisely planned, leaving scant room for error, particularly unexpected ones. Now a small mishap careened into major disaster as precious moments slipped away. Possibly another day's worth of oxygen remained, and then it would be over. The time marks that earlier carried tremendous anticipation now factored dread and doom as each second ticked by ominously. Armstrong and Aldrin rapidly faced the possibility of becoming the moon's first permanent residents. Even if some sort of makeshift solution were concocted within the few extra hours of reserve oxygen possessed, if it did not work to perfection the mission would still fail. An orchestration of exacting events was dependent upon the precise operation of the missing switch. The engine must ignite to immediate, full power to attain escape velocity from the moon. The engine must then run at full power for a specified time to achieve the requisite, inflexible launch trajectory. If any point was minutely off, the rendezvous location with the command ship or the window of time to meet it would be missed. That would be it. No ride home and no second chance.

After the astronauts had quietly radioed Houston Space Center about the problem, teams of scientists raced urgently to their mockup of the module and began racking their brains for options. To duplicate the dire situation on the moon, they hurriedly whacked the ignition switch from the control panel. Aldrin and Armstrong continued to brainstorm for answers in their cramped, limited quarters on the moon, hoping the *Eagle* would not become the first lunar tomb.

With the switch unusable and the cavity narrow what could reach in to flip the metal strip to initiate the engines? At one point in the mass of questions and consultations, a suggestion was made regarding one small tool still in the lunar module, but being a long-shot, it was hoped better options would arise. Whatever the final solution, there would be only one opportunity to attempt it. The answer if it could truly work would be revealed at the crucial ignition point to blast off from the lunar surface. And at that juncture, well, no do-overs. Moment by moment dragged by filled with tension, anxiety and anticipation, wondering, would the launch sequence bring salvation or ultimate tragedy? The seconds continued to tick onward...

Since that pivotal moment would not arrive for some hours, the astronauts were ordered to get sleep. With virtually no space to move, Armstrong tethered himself above the ascent engine hatch. Aldrin curled up on the minimal floor space in a fitful attempt at rest. Sensors monitoring Armstrong's heart and pulse back on earth belied that sleep could not overcome his restless mind.

Above them, *Columbia* commander, Michael Collins pondered his role in their situation. If the LEM engine didn't fire, there was nothing he could do to rescue them. Collins would simply have to return to earth alone, leaving Armstrong and Aldrin to die on the surface of the moon.

Finally at 124:21:33 into the mission, eleven and a half long, stressful hours following the initial discovery of the broken switch, the time arrived to initiate the launch from the lunar crust. The two lunar explorers continued their perfunctory readiness checks until at last Houston called out: "You're cleared for take off."

The makeshift tool was carefully slipped into the broken slot and twisted…

VOOM!

The 3,500 lb. thrust rocket blasted to life. The tiny spacecraft shot out of the launching frame into the blackness of the lunar sky, picking up speed from an initial 30 mph after 10 seconds, then accelerating rapidly to a bullet speed of 1,800 mph. It needed to run steady and strong for the next seven minutes.

And it did. The rendezvous was achieved. Three days later the mission to land a man on the moon ended triumphantly back on earth.

The vital "tool" for this delicate moment proved to be Fisher's sleek metal space pen. The tubular metal housing of the pen offered the conductive material, and the tensile strength with just the right diameter to slip into the void left by the destroyed toggle switch, bridge the circuits and successfully ignite the engines.

The lunar mission averted tragedy and achieved success at a critical juncture not because a pen substituted as a toggle, but because decades earlier an individual with no idea the role his quest for excellence would play on the world stage, strove to insure that the product of his labors reflected his best efforts.

Hundreds of millions never knew of the life and death dilemma occurring a quarter of a million miles away in space…least of all Paul Fisher, the quiet Los Angeles businessman who had ultimately provided the solution that saved the most monumental day in modern history.

Striving for excellence reaches far beyond us, contributing in ways we would never imagine.

36
Working the Bugs Out
1901 C.E.

Focused on a narrow isthmus called Panama, the attention of the world turned toward Central America in 1880. One of the greatest engineering undertakings of the age, a waterway linking the Atlantic and the Pacific Oceans had been proposed. France confidently declared herself as the world leader that would successfully complete a series of locks and canals through Panama. The project would revolutionize world commerce, shipping and travel by trimming 9,000 nautical miles from the only known East-West route around the tip of South America. The coup would also secure French global prestige and lucrative fortune for decades to come.

France placed in charge Ferdinand de Lesseps, the architect of their earlier and hugely successful Suez Canal project in Egypt. He exuberantly undertook the challenge to plan and create the new shipping canal through the Isthmus of Panama. Backed with the capital of thousands of confident, high profile investors, de Lesseps assuredly looked on the harsh environment of Central America with an air of aplomb.

Despite the initial élan, de Lesseps and his workforce of 10,000 encountered immediate dilemma and quandaries. Unlike the dry, arid, open, flat conditions of the Egyptian desert, the Panamanian jungle rebuffed the attempts to tame it. Much more than a steaming tangle of dense vegetation, the region unfolded as a continuing nightmare of rugged, hilly terrain, impenetrable rain forests, quagmire soil and dangerous creatures; a land terrorized by earthquakes, monsoons, massive flooding and the specters of widespread disease and death in the form of Yellow Fever and Malaria.

The intense environment, resulting in desertion, suicides plus thousands of deaths from disease and accidents, quickly dampened, dulled, and soon quashed the French workforce's passion for the project. Further problems appeared in the form of inept, largely unworkable engineering plans based on misconceptions. Following some preliminary excavation, progress slowed to a halt.

Back in Europe, the French news media uncovered the project to be riddled with corruption on a grand scale entailing over $265 million dollars. Enveloped in an embarrassing, national scandal regarding financial abuses and gross mishandling of the venture, the French withdrew from Panama, abandoning everything. The massive machines left behind quietly rusted; posing like herds of fossilized dinosaurs amidst the steaming, dense jungle that proceeded to slowly and irresistibly envelope and devour them.

What was once world awe had shifted to intense scrutiny and widespread criticism. France found herself humiliated before the eyes of the entire world.

In 1901, twenty years following France's initial declaration, world attention turned toward Theodore Roosevelt, the new president of the United States. He boldly touted American ingenuity and a "can do" attitude, promising to renew construction and secure swift completion of the canal. True to his word the Panama Canal project consummated and opened in record time amidst great enthusiasm, grand fanfare and prominent notice that the United States had arrived on the world stage.

Why had the United States proved successful while France had not? Competence and organization? Not really. The American campaign emerged as organizationally jumbled and as corrupt as the French effort. There surfaced just as much confusion, chicanery, crookedness and politics gumming up the works. However someone recognized another issue beyond the mass of procedural problems.

This key person in the canal process responsible for its ultimate success was U.S. Army General William Gorgas. When General Gorgas commandeered the canal project he immediately directed every resource toward engineering one goal…health. Dr. Gorgas happened to be a military physician.

The United States gained control of the situation and victory in the project, not due to superior mechanical engineering or strength, but because it pursued, and challenged issues far beyond the obvious. The team figured out how to engineer the restriction of bug infestation, and the reduction of disease. During canal construction under French management over two thousand workers lost their lives, almost exclusively to tropical disease. Fear and discouragement took toll on the remaining healthy men.

In preparation for the U.S. project, Dr. Gorgas tested, and proved that mosquitoes transmitted both, Yellow Fever and Malaria. He then devised ways to control all three of the bugs that had hampered France's construction effort – insect, illness and attitude. With a good dose of education and inoculation, the U.S. completed the Panama Canal, losing only 137 men from illness.

Often the answer to our challenges lies in matters not immediately obvious.

37
Center of Attention
1814 C. E.

The creaking wooden door closed with the snap of the latch, signaling the departure of the immensely important visitor. It had been a simple request, but it set renowned French painter Jean-Baptiste Isabey into dismay, realizing that political faction had once more thrust itself into his life and livelihood. The middle aged artist sighed heavily and sank into a chair, staring disconsolately at the large blank canvas and empty sketch papers scattered before him. Neither offered solace nor solution for the commissioned and celebrated work expected of him. Fame indeed has its price. Perhaps it now loomed too high for Isabey.

1787 opened with Jean-Baptiste painting, beautiful, detailed miniatures on tiny snuff boxes. His intricately embellished coffers suddenly discovered favor with King Louis XVI and his Queen, Marie Antoinette. Soon everyone who was anyone in France had to have at least one of his objet d'art. In short time, the artist found himself called to stay at the palace of Versailles while engaged in the royal consignments awarded him. Among the reigning aristocracy in France, ownership of large portraiture paintings by Isabey became the rage in high society.

Fame came fast and furious, but in those days, so did radical political change. In 1789 the French Revolution exploded in heinous anarchy and unthinkable mob violence lusting for the death of the aristocracy. The Reign of Terror quickly ended many lives and livelihoods through mere association with the monarchy. The rampant French governmental upheaval evolved, bringing widespread death via the guillotine to royalty and those connected with them. Isabey, anxious for his life, laid low, evading the angry fray.

Financially desperate, and in near threadbare conditions in 1791, Isabey's path crossed that of a publisher associated with the revolutionary party's new National Assembly. He brought Isabey's impressive artistic talent to their attention. Rather than the retribution Isabey feared, they instead commissioned him to paint their official portraits…all 228 of them.

For nine years the National Assembly sought to control the frenzied chaos in France without success. Finally with military precision, a 1799 coup d'etat swept Napoleon Bonaparte into power. Napoleon's new government established and enforced strict regulations to convene order; eliminating the bedlam…and those associated with it. Vulnerable for a third time, Isabey stressed over the safety of his family and himself.

With the national turmoil settled, the new ruling class turned focus toward the aesthetic attributes of life. Napoleon's wife, Josephine elevated and advanced the appreciation for fine art. Once again, Jean-Baptiste skirted his earlier liaisons, arising to new eminence as an artist, and as family friend to Napoleon and Josephine. He even earned "beloved uncle" status among the Emperor's children. In 1804 Isabey orchestrated the official coronation proclaiming Napoleon Emperor of the French Empire. As a result, the new upper echelon along with military leaders clamored to claim the haut monde of owning an original portrait by the prestigious Isabey.

Napoleon's grand ambition for his French empire immersed all of Europe in warfare. For the next decade French armies invaded, occupied and overwhelmed the continent, tearing governments asunder, installing vassal states, wreaking destruction and imposing tyranny from Spain and Portugal in the west reaching eastward all the way to Moscow. After years of devastating and debilitating hostilities against the nations of Europe, Napoleon and his massive armies were finally decimated, driven back to France and defeated. In April of 1814, Napoleon abdicated, and was thrust into exile; his army dissolved. Many linked to his reign simply disappeared.

Stigmatized by his affiliations and dogged once more by political faction to undergo feast then famine, Isabey's life and career again balanced on the cusp. With no further patrons in Paris, Jean-Baptiste initiated a self-imposed exile to Austria.

Regime ideals and tides turned and churned a fourth time. Now the former leaders of the nations released from Napoleon's tyranny, including royalty, diplomats, generals, and heads of state emerged, and agreed to meet in Austria for discussion on the reestablishment of Europe's countries.

An illustrious world event, the famed 1814 Congress of Vienna brought together an assembly of the most renowned and important individuals on the European continent. Their purpose: to reestablish governments and national borders in the aftermath of Napoleon's suzerain. The Congress produced a political celebrity showcase; glitterati of the powerful and the proud. With a gaggle of world newspaper writers in attendance, every action, every nuance, every scandalous snub or tiff served to fuel the fires of intrigue and news. Historically, the eminence of this event could not be denied.

In the years prior to photography, presentation and preservation of pivotal events were depicted on canvas by a selected artist. The Congress of Vienna from April, 1814 to June, 1815 marked an epic occasion. This distinguished gathering with its merited and immense attention required visual commemoration by a master.

The recipient of this privilege for the high-profile and prestigious task was none other than French artist Jean-Baptiste Isabey, living in Vienna and plucked from his seclusion. Isabey may have hoped the opportunity to paint a group portrait of international leaders for peace might once and for all eliminate any political rancor and ill-fated ghosts that filled his past.

But just moments earlier, the most powerful military and political figure in all Europe had stopped by for an informal visit. England's Duke of Wellington, the only man who repeatedly defeated Napoleon's fierce armies, and an individual destined to become Prime Minister of the British Empire, sought to make a small request of the artist. Like others of the period, Wellington recognized the current and future importance of the painting and perspective it would leave. He lobbied Isabey to paint him in the center of it as the focus of attention.

How could Isabey say no to a man of Wellington's caliber and acclaim? Even as Isabey courteously agreed to Wellington's request the painter caught his breath when his heart froze. Just days before, as the artist quietly prepared sketches in his studio, there had been another unassuming knock upon his door. In responding, Isabey found himself face to face with the renowned Charles François Talleyrand, the most vaunted French diplomat of the time. This distinguished individual and fellow countryman had survived the political upheavals of the French monarchy, the French Revolution, the Reign of Terror, and Napoleon's rule. Now he evolved into the representative of France's soon-to-be restored king.

Talleyrand's visit to his fellow countryman amounted to a simple suggestion. Since he, Talleyrand, represented negotiations for Jean-Baptist's native country and carried years of prominence as a politician of immeasurable importance, he should occupy the center of the painting. Jean-Baptiste, a fellow Frenchman, respectfully agreed to the idea. And Talleyrand left the meeting pleased. As had the Duke of Wellington moments earlier, having secured that same promise from Isabey to place the Englishman in the center.

The artist found himself in an impossible predicament. He would be painting Europe's greatest collection of war heroes, ambassadors, royalty, and politicians ever gathered in one place. The whole world would be watching the reactions of the nobility to praise or criticize Isabey's work. As the only official artist, anything he did that displeased these luminaries would be trumpeted across the map of Europe.

Isabey reflected over the turbulence that political disfavor had inflicted upon his career. Deliberating on this situation Isabey could foresee once more on the horizon the potential ruination of his repute. His dilemma presented a picture-perfect disaster. How could he possibly produce a painting that would allow for the two important men in his work to be satisfied, particularly since both had been promised the center of the portrait?

Later, when the highly anticipated canvas premiered before the assembled heads of Europe, a hush swept across the crowd as Isabey unveiled his work. Within moments it became clear that both Wellington and Talleyrand approved, exceptionally pleased with the masterpiece. Each found himself highly honored by his placement in the composition.

What had Isabey done to accomplish their universal satisfaction and admiration?

The painting depicts a large meeting room, crowded with twenty three important diplomats and dignitaries from across the continent. Seated and standing around a table with chairs, the various men pose, posture and gesture. An elaborate chair sits in the center of the painting, comfortably occupied by Talleyrand. To the far right of the painting, the Duke of Wellington is seen entering the room...and all eyes in the room, including Talleyrand's are upon the Duke. Talleyrand occupied the center; Wellington occupied the center of attention. And Jean-Baptiste Isabey occupied the center of admiration.

Isabey's years with political strife and violence, where only one viewpoint could rule, had enabled him to see there can be different perspectives do exist; the tool that he used to create a unifying solution for the problem at hand. How well we could do to learn the same.

38
Sleeping Dragon
Circa 230 C.E.

In the timeless history of China, Zhuge Liang demonstrated time and again to be one of her greatest generals. This brilliant leader directed the Kingdom of Shu military during a legendary period regarded as The Three Kingdoms. Through his ingenious strategies and uncommon cleverness, Zhuge Liang had earned a venerable reputation for defeating armies many times his own force's size and strength. Garnering the nickname, "The Sleeping Dragon", his abilities proved so compelling that he gained prominent mention in the Taoist religious canons for his consummate skill to "defeat great armies with nothingness". Liang's opponents viewed his ingenuity as more powerful than any powerful, armed force.

Following one successful yet extended military campaign, Liang rewarded his tired army by sending them several days journey to a secret camp for rest and recuperation. He decided to take a short respite of his own, two days' travel in the opposite direction, retreating to a small, isolated, friendly village. The tiny, walled town warmly welcomed the familiar, famous general along with his small bodyguard of 100 trusted men. It would be a quiet and peaceful rest.

A short while after arriving, Zhuge Liang's sentinels rushed to him in abject alarm! The massive enemy militia of Liang's most mortal enemy, Sima Yi, rapidly approached; an army numbering over 150,000 strong. Sima Yi had battled Zhuge Liang dozens of times. This opposing general proved well versed in Liang's crafty methods and reputation for military shock and surprise. Obviously a well planted spy had alerted Yi to Liang's vulnerable situation.

Zhuge Liang didn't bother with the obvious question of identifying who had betrayed him and how it was done. That would rank of little consequence now.

The situation fared desperately hopeless. Isolated with only a handful of men to defend him, Liang and his trusted men would undoubtedly be summarily captured, brutally tortured and viciously executed by the cruel Sima Yi.

The invaders would be at the gates in an hour. Liang quickly surmised that his best weapon remained as sharp as any sword. How to use it? What tools stood at his disposal? Swiftly he designed a plan.

Liang ordered his troops to complete a list of four tasks:

- Send the townsfolk to hide within their homes and take their livestock inside with them. Remain there and stay quiet.
- Remove all flags and banners from the town's walls. Decorations and standards identified town populations, inherent trades and businesses along with any visiting militia. Liang wanted no clues as to the size or strength of his visiting force, or that anyone even lived within the walls.
- Throw open the city gates. Show absolutely no defense. Show no signs of life.
- Liang's soldiers were to hide, and not reveal themselves until his signal.

Upon giving these orders, Zhuge Liang donned a Taoist priestly robe, and then took with him a large pot of incense, a chair and his lute, a popular stringed musical instrument, to the top of the city wall. There upon the flat, stone arch directly above the gates, he chose to make his stand. Situating himself in the most obvious, open and vulnerable spot he could find, Liang settled in. He lit the incense, arranged himself comfortably upon the chair, took up his lute…and began to strum and sing.

Within a few minutes of scanning the horizon, he spied the enemy, a seemingly endless phalanx of soldiers moving rapidly toward the town. He continued strumming and singing song after song, pretending not to notice the massive, hostile formation advancing directly towards him.

At the command of Liang's nemesis, Sima Yi, the innumerable rows and huge divisions of soldiers halted within a stone's throw of the gates. Abruptly the enemy general recognized his adversary sitting atop the wall. Yi rode his horse to the head of his troops, stopped, then silently observed. He studied and weighed the strange situation that lay before him. No sign of soldiers anywhere. An apparently deserted town with gates flung open. It begged his approach. Yet most disconcerting, his hated enemy casually seated alone and completely vulnerable atop the city wall, absolutely ignoring the vast army arrayed before him while calmly crooning merry songs...as if to goad Sima Yi to launch an attack.

Yi's lieutenants moved to his side and strongly urged him to move forward; take the town, capture his forlorn opponent, win the day. But Sima Yi had been beaten more than once by the craftiness of this unpretentious man before him. He knew Liang's deserved reputation all too well. Even with seasoned experience fighting against Liang, Sima Yi could not fathom the situation displayed before him. Could this be some kind a trap? Yi held his men back, spending more time studying Liang on the wall. Liang himself never acknowledged the army or the general leading it. He simply played on, coy and completely unconcerned.

The longer Sima Yi hesitated, the more tentative and unsure he became. Moments dragged. Then Sima Yi suddenly ordered an about face. The invading hordes hastily retreated from whence they came.

Once again, Zhuge Liang bested a massive army with the greatest weapon at his disposal: His well earned reputation. Liang had defeated the great force with emptiness, turning his opponent's own assumptions and doubts against himself to drive the entire enemy army back.

In the present world, battles confront us every day. Often the odds are overwhelming and one feels seemingly defenseless. Perhaps the strongest weapon in any arsenal is the one an individual can best develop...a strong repute.

With a strong reputation, one can win before even beginning.

39
Sermon Walking
1949 C.E.

The excitement among the mass of press and people seemed nearly palatable at the Chicago railway station that afternoon in 1949. The great city had enjoyed its share of notables and dignitaries over the years, but few individuals' renown and respect compared to the internationally known philosopher and humanitarian arriving today. No popular celebrity, film icon, world or religious leader elicited the attention and focus generated by Dr. Albert Schweitzer. Perceiving him as a renaissance man for the 20th century, the world press hung upon his every word and action.

Dr. Albert Schweitzer had risen over the years to reign amidst the most influential individuals of the age. As a philosopher, his writings on ethics and "reverence for life" provided a new cornerstone for leaders in government and business to regard people's rights and public service. Hailed since 1906 as one of Germany's greatest theologians, his treatise on Jesus Christ in the New Testament set a new tone in Christian thinking worldwide. A distinguished concert organist, Schweitzer's musical genius redefined the perception of Johann Sebastian Bach's complex compositions and how they should be, and continue to be performed. As a builder of church organs, Schweitzer's complexity of mind and personal skill revealed themselves through the minute details and complicated designs of the organs he created.

In 1905 following years of noted successes in Europe, Schweitzer decided to become a medical missionary. After enduring eight grueling years of medical school, he graduated in 1913, nearly forty years old. He moved to Africa, giving up everything. His dedicated commitment to the people of that continent made him an enigma; perhaps imposing his greatest fame.

With brilliant opportunities beckoning him, Dr. Schweitzer left the lofty halls of academia and prestige to pursue his calling, serving the poor in Africa by establishing a hospital in Gabon and ministering to the black tribes. For thirty-six years and through two world wars, Dr. Schweitzer remained devoted to his cause and passionate for race relations. To self-fund his efforts, he occasionally returned to Europe, lecturing and performing concerts.

And such was the situation in 1949. In Schweitzer's long and storied life, this would be his one and only trip to America. The celebrated doctor had traveled the length and breadth of the United States by train for well over a month, making appearances, giving speeches, accepting accolades, and raising funds. Chicago weighed in as the final stop before his departure for Europe from New York within the week.

Albert Schweitzer's Chicago arrival did not disappoint. The powerful train slowed majestically as it entered the station. Shrill and demanding whistles announced his advent. Steam blasted and hissed as the massive wheels braked to a stop. The anticipation heightened to a crescendo as the respected gentleman appeared above the crowd at the doorway of the Pullman car. Preparing to take the steps down to the platform, the distinguished icon with his rich, white hair and full moustache, cut a commanding figure with regal bearing and six foot four inch stature.

At the first sighting of him, illuminated by the storm of flashing and popping newspaper camera bulbs, the crowd roared with excitement. High-elected officials seeking to jockey for position to launch into their prepared welcoming speeches were duly ignored by the throngs enthralled by Schweitzer.

Smiling, the guest of honor humbly acknowledged their attention. Pausing before stepping down, the direction of his gaze suddenly shifted, looking beyond the pressing crowd. Hesitating briefly, he politely asked if the well-wishers would please excuse him for a moment. Descending from the train to the platform he quickly strode through the suddenly silent, quizzical and respectfully parting throngs until he moved clear of the masses. Coming to the side of an elderly black woman struggling with two large suitcases, Schweitzer offered a warm smile, picked up the bags and personally escorted her to the bus. After loading the suitcases into the luggage bay, and gently helping the older lady board the steps, he cordially chatted for a moment and cheerfully wished her a safe and enjoyable journey.

Returning again to the gathered throngs, who stood dumbfounded, he sincerely apologized: "I am very sorry to have kept you waiting."

The stunned silence of the press and gathered throngs spoke volumes. The illustrious Dr. Albert Schweitzer had stopped to aid an anonymous, ordinary black woman. Few, if any, areas of the United States lived with such racial open-mindedness. "Jim Crow" laws and "separate but equal" rhetoric permeated the legal system. At this point in time, overt racial prejudice, outright hatred and severe double standards saturated society. Public acceptance of this biased thinking had existed for nearly one hundred years following the American Civil War. Few cared or dared even broach the subject, much less take active steps to change it.

For those assembled that day, the world-esteemed Dr. Schweitzer had humbly displayed his core belief in a simple, unassuming and breathtaking manner.

One member of the reception committee summed it up well. With quiet awe and admiration he commented to the reporter beside him, "That's the first time I ever saw a sermon walking."

What does ones' own walk say to the world, each and every day?

40
Blank Pages
1349 C.E.

On a glorious spring afternoon, there arose a quiet and serene moment as the warm sunset cast a golden glow across the sparkling, lush green hills of Kilkenny, Ireland. A solitary monk paused in his writing to gaze one final time from his monastery window and contemplate the breathtaking beauty spread before him. Musing to himself, he never anticipated that this would be the way the world would appear…when it all ended.

Brother Clynn quickly returned from his momentary daydream to resume his furiously paced writing, chronicling the end of the world. The task has fallen to him since he remains alone as the last person alive. And he already knows the cold, bony fingers of Death are quietly beckoning him; clutching at him. Time has grown short.

And certainly, Brother Clynn is correct. Since 1346, one third of the known world had died. The dreaded Black Plague, capable of killing a perfectly healthy person within hours, had swept across Asia, along North Africa and through Europe with lightening speed between 1346 and 1350. Undiminished, it crossed the English Channel. England, Scotland and Ireland were felled. Even the isolated Northern enclaves of Norway, Greenland and Iceland lay ravaged. In just four years almost every corner of the world had been decimated. Truly the world was ending. And those very few who still survived wondered what kind of world remained to live in…

No one remained who understood or pursued the sciences and medicine. Education had evaporated, and with it written language. The great structures, the cathedrals and castles stood unfinished. With architects and craftsmen gone, both veteran and novice, no one possessed the knowledge, skill or understanding to construct buildings and furnishings, or even use of the tools to fashion them.

With no one left to tend the fields, crops failed. Farms and pastures lay fallow and forgotten. Widespread starvation reigned. Economies collapsed for gold and silver are worthless when basic sustenance cannot be obtained.

The order of social structure, governments and the church had collapsed. The loss of royalty, judges, clergy, lawmakers and protectors

129

had brought chaos. Few leaders remained across the known world. Justice, organization and morality shifted into endless lawlessness and anarchy. The fabric of civilization had been rent and torn asunder.

There existed nothing but death. The animals died as quickly as the humans. Corpses littered the land since people and animals died faster and in greater numbers than anyone could manage. Mass burial or even wholesale cremation could not handle the volume. Almost like the flood of Noah, the wave of death seemed to wipe clean the earth, leaving no creature untouched in its path.

Brother Clynn, the forlorn, lonely monk, sat absolutely alone in a corner of this maelstrom of mortality. The beautiful, sun filled countryside lay supremely silent; devoid of people or even the common animals. Brother Clynn's cloistered world had also been swept clean. The last of the brothers died an excruciating death just hours ago. Now, his monastery devoid of any other human sounds, Brother Clynn heard the distant echoes of the all too familiar funeral dirge; a constant companion over these last months. But this time it sings in his mind alone. It mourns for him. The icy grip of the Grim Reaper tightens as the disease quickly ravages him.

Knowing his end was near; Bother Clynn penned his last words, chronicling the end of existence:

"And lest notable acts should perish with time,
and pass out of the memory of future generations, I, as if
amongst the dead, waiting 'til death do come, have put
into writing truthfully what I have heard and verified.
And that the writing may not perish with the scribe, and
the work fail with the laborer, I add parchment to
continue it, if by chance anyone may be left in the future
and any child of Adam may escape this pestilence and
continue the work thus commenced."
~ Brother John Clynn, Friar

Next to his journal, he neatly placed five pieces of blank parchment. And at this point in a strange mix of conclusion and surprise, Brother Clynn scrawled a final notation: "Here the author appears to have died."

It is a grim story. Yet even amidst this horrible carnage, the immense depression and the massive toll on humanity, hope existed.

The blank pages spoke volumes. For the presence of Brother Clynn's neat stack of clean parchment meant that even in death, alone and forlorn, he still believed. He did not understand how it could possibly be, but there still existed distinct hope that somehow, somewhere, some way, another might survive to come and finish the tale; continue the journey, carry on the work.

At the end of the day, is there hope left behind for yourself and others to discover?

41
Windows of Remembrance
July, 2000 C.E.

In the early morning hours of August 2, 1944, a squadron of American P-51 fighter planes on patrol just north of Paris roared over the Nazi-occupied town of Remy, France. They spied a target: an 18-car munitions train the Germans had hidden and heavily camouflaged outside the farmlands encircling the small, rural community.

The planes of the American 383rd fighter group swooped in, striking ferociously at the concealed train. Their intent: destroy it. A storm of bullets raked over the rail cars as the planes rolled, banked, and dove, making repeated strafing runs, again and again to attack the huge train. German soldiers on the ground scattered under the withering aerial bombardment, many scurried to hide under the train. Some sporadically turned to shoot ineffectively with small arms fire at the planes. The occasional staccato of a single heavy machine gun responded to the attack.

Wheeling about once more, the fighters flew a final low-level run over the rail station, achieving their objective. The Mustangs' blazing .50 caliber machine guns struck a provision of nitroglycerin. Instantly there erupted a tremendous, massive explosion. The train, stockpiled with explosive warheads, artillery, and volatile nitroglycerin for rocket fuel, completely disintegrated. Strewn among the fiery wreckage, more than 100 Nazi soldiers lay dead. In place of the train station lay a huge trench, ten feet deep, forty feet wide and several hundred feet in length.

Nearly a mile from the eruption, the concussion of the blast impacted the entire little village of Remy, leaving homes damaged and roofs ripped away. The rural town's singular icon, a small 13th Century church violently shuddered in the reverberation. The powerful shock wave on the ancient structure blew the revered chapel's seven hundred year old, beautifully ornate stained glass windows from their casements, totally obliterating them.

The Americans felt the shock of loss as well. Turning to look at the aftermath of the explosion, they saw an empty position in their formation. The mass of hurling, burning debris scattered from the blast had sliced off a partial tail section of the P-51 plane piloted by Lt. Houston Lee Braly, Jr. from Brady, Texas. The flaming fighter plane screamed low across the landscape, directly toward the hamlet. Braly struggled to swerve his doomed aircraft, barely avoiding the town and its people. The craft instead plowed heavily into a nearby farmyard, killing the twenty-two year old Texan.

Despite the explosion's devastation resulting from the Allied raid, the French natives knew the Americans were fighting…and dying…to liberate them from the intense Nazi tyranny. Like many Frenchmen across the occupied nation, they in turn, willingly risked their very lives to protect and honor the American pilots – alive or dead. The Germans knew it too. Throughout France, they had threatened death and serious reprisals to anyone who involved themselves with the Allies in any fashion.

On that day in Remy, while the Germans occupied themselves with their severe, and wide-spread casualties amidst the destroyed train wreckage, Maria, a young sixteen year old, defied the recent Nazi death threats. Arriving first at the crash site, she struggled to remove and recover Braly's remains from the wrecked aircraft. Maria risked her life in a daring effort for the dead American flyer. Hazarding the flames, fumes, leaking fuel and ammunition in the dangerous, smoldering wreckage, Maria strained to painstakingly pull the American's remains from the debris. Inch by agonizing inch, she dragged the battered and bloody body out of the crumpled cockpit through shattered glass, twisted metal and burning electrical wiring. Once clear of the smoking hulk of his aircraft, she quickly opened and unfurled the airman's unused parachute. Pushing his remains to it, she rolled his body to wrap it in the chute. Other villagers reached the scene and knowing the Germans would soon be swarming the area, struggled to hastily hide Braly's body in a nearby farmer's stable.

Later under cover of darkness, while avoiding Nazi patrols, the locals again risked their safety to stealthily shuffle the pilot to the hamlet's damaged church and its small cemetery. A small, quiet funeral was held by the local priest with a couple of townsfolk. Then Braly's remains were placed in an obscure, hastily prepared grave. They marked the grave with a small shard of the Texan's propeller.

Thus began a mission that ended 55 years later…

In later years, the army pilots of the 383rd fighter group and the townsfolk grew to know each other. The remembrance of friendship and appreciation eventually saw Remy, France and Brady, Texas become sister cities. Grandchildren now accompanied the aged pilots on their occasional pilgrimages to Remy to visit and recall times past. Braly's body long ago had been returned to Texas, but his buddies' spirit and focus remained with this quaint French village and a commitment the pilots sought to fulfill.

Remy had always been a very poor community. Although they survived the war, they were unable to replace the cherished windows of their beloved St. Denis church. Filled with respect for the kindness of the French townsfolk for their fallen compatriot, the aged American pilots, now in their seventies and eighties, realized their final mission. They diligently set to work, eventually managing to raise $200,000 to replace the seven windows in the Church; the windows the town could not afford to reinstate. The magnificent new stained glass windows were designed and cast by a French artist with their installation completed in July of 2000.

And finally, the 383rd fighter squadron had completed its final mission.

It may take half a lifetime to fulfill a commitment, but remaining faithful to one's commitments can bring a lifetime to fulfillment.
Public or personal, openly made or internally vowed…
are there some promises unfulfilled in your life?
Now might just be the best time to return and complete them.

42
And the Aftermath
1975 C.E.

On the upper campus of California State University, Long Beach, the 1975 installation of a new sculpture had drawn agitated indignation from the college students. The $40,000 project avowed to be a remembrance of the recently culminated Vietnam conflict. Its creator, noted artist Tom Van Sant, had entitled the icon "War Memorial", claiming the piece graphically detailed the aftermath of war and its violence.

Like a severely gashed wound upon the soft, grassy gathering area of the campus, the prominent, intimidating and ghastly eyesore loomed over 8 feet tall and nearly 7 feet across. Ripped from a decommissioned warship, the monstrosity was a huge, ugly, shapeless hunk of gray, heavy armor-plating about 4 inches thick. Obtained from the China Lake military firing range in the California desert, the imposing Navy ship scrap had been severely impacted by a large, howitzer artillery round. The resultant explosion and heat proved so intense that it brutally melted the immense steel plating, wrinkling and tearing it like a piece of paper in the instant before it cooled. Now filled with twisted, gnarled, ragged ruptures, the armored plate captured the moment of extreme violence, freezing it for all time; a searing reminder to all who viewed it. On the ground behind the demolished steel shield, representing its expulsion by the blast's violent assault, lays the missing, twisted shard of metal. A moment of horror and brutality as strongly graphic and symbolic in its destruction as the gaping wound conflicts can leave in human lives.

The hideous hole left by the shard hung nearly centered in the huge, thick piece of plating, a broad, ripped aperture that grabbed attention; mute, graphic testimony of the brute force expelled by the exploding artillery shell. Yet along the lower, jagged section of the hole, also almost centrally located, the artist had placed a small, bronze dove, comfortably perched, watching the world go by, oblivious to its roosting place and how the perch came to be.

The student body saw the ugly, mutilated metal memorial as a waste of university funding, abuse of precious green space, and recognition for a war that others preferred to forget. Campus newspaper editorials and loud vocal derision claimed no artistic merit or value existed in mounting a couple of battered and misshapen steel plates on a one foot high by ten foot square base of bland concrete.

Time passed, as it always does, and before everyone's eyes, the sculpture began to change. The stark, revolting horror of the splintered warship's imposing armor plating began to disappear. Leaf by leaf, strand by strand, soft green tendrils of creeping vines, carefully planted at the base of the sculpture by Van Sant during installation began to grow. Plantings of hope, vision and promise, they gently wove their way over the shocking horror…caressing and enveloping the torn steel. Soon only the small bronze dove, the symbol of peace and healing, remained visible. Peace, tarnished but triumphant. Van Sant's genius and message had unfolded, and today the imposing sculpture resembles a giant, lush green hedge encircling a small, peaceful dove. Only upon close inspection does one realize what lies beneath.

It is said art imitates nature. Life can gouge and gash, piercing the heart and very soul with seemingly well aimed, or even random missile blows. Van Sant's sculpture stands as a reminder that when inner peace resides, Providence can take the ugliest, most painful of scars and eventually soften them with time, creating something unique and beautiful in its place.

Southern California author Scott Ski holds a nationally accredited degree in broadcast journalism from California State University, Long Beach. His continuing education included subsequent coursework at Biola University, Talbot Theological Seminary, and UCLA, plus certification in technical writing from California State University, Dominguez Hills, and creative writing through California State University, Long Beach.

Dogged and Determined
Scott's earlier book of personal experiences with dog rescue, remains popular with dog lovers and animal rescue organizations worldwide. It is also available at ScottSki.net.

Every moment of life,
every square inch of our world,
brims with insight to discover and share.
All we have to do is diligently seek it out.

Thank you for having taken the time and looked here.

Always Seeking...
Scott Ski

Printed in the United States
200445BV00003BB/22-42/A